Cowboy Cookie Mix

1 1/3 C. old-fashioned oats
1/2 C. brown sugar
1/2 C. sugar
1/3 C. chopped pecans
3/4 C. semi-sweet chocolate
   chips
1 1/3 C. all-purpose flour
1 tsp. baking powder
1 tsp. baking soda
1/4 tsp. salt

Layer the ingredients in the order given into a wide-mouth 1-quart canning jar. Pack each layer in place before adding the next ingredient.

Attach a gift tag with the mixing and baking directions.

Cowboy Cookies

Makes 2 1/2 to 3 dozen

1 jar Cowboy Cookie Mix
1/2 C. butter or margarine,
   melted
1 egg
1 tsp. vanilla

Preheat the oven to 350°F. In a medium bowl, cream butter, egg and vanilla. Add the Cowboy Cookie Mix. Stir until the mixture is well blended. You may need to use your hands to finish mixing. Shape dough into walnut sized balls. Place dough balls 2 inches apart on a greased cookie sheet. Bake for 11 to 13 minutes. Transfer to wire racks to cool.

Cowboy Cookies
Makes 2 1/2 to 3 dozen

1 jar Cowboy Cookie Mix
1/2 C. butter or margarine, melted

1 egg
1 tsp. vanilla

Preheat the oven to 350°F. In a medium bowl, cream butter, egg and vanilla. Add the Cowboy Cookie Mix. Stir until the mixture is well blended. You may need to use your hands to finish mixing. Shape dough into walnut sized balls. Place dough balls 2 inches apart on a greased cookie sheet. Bake for 11 to 13 minutes. Transfer to wire racks to cool.

Cowboy Cookies
Makes 2 1/2 to 3 dozen

1 jar Cowboy Cookie Mix
1/2 C. butter or margarine, melted

1 egg
1 tsp. vanilla

Preheat the oven to 350°F. In a medium bowl, cream butter, egg and vanilla. Add the Cowboy Cookie Mix. Stir until the mixture is well blended. You may need to use your hands to finish mixing. Shape dough into walnut sized balls. Place dough balls 2 inches apart on a greased cookie sheet. Bake for 11 to 13 minutes. Transfer to wire racks to cool.

Cowboy Cookies
Makes 2 1/2 to 3 dozen

1 jar Cowboy Cookie Mix
1/2 C. butter or margarine, melted

1 egg
1 tsp. vanilla

Preheat the oven to 350°F. In a medium bowl, cream butter, egg and vanilla. Add the Cowboy Cookie Mix. Stir until the mixture is well blended. You may need to use your hands to finish mixing. Shape dough into walnut sized balls. Place dough balls 2 inches apart on a greased cookie sheet. Bake for 11 to 13 minutes. Transfer to wire racks to cool.

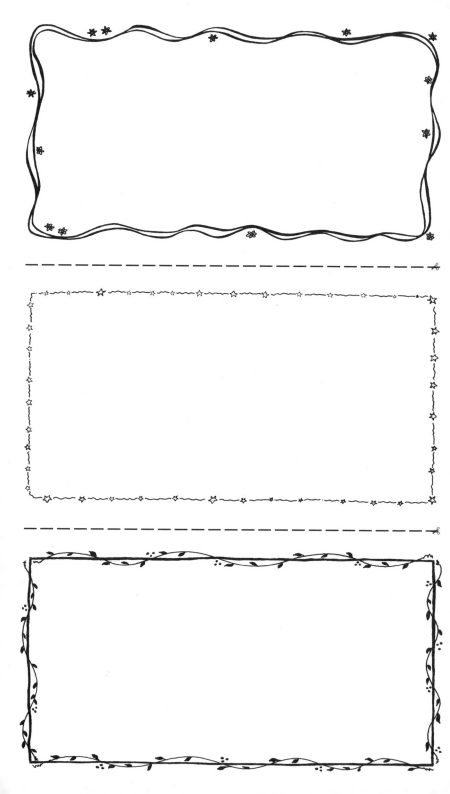

Cowboy Cookies
Makes 2 1/2 to 3 dozen

1 jar Cowboy Cookie Mix
1/2 C. butter or margarine,
   melted

1 egg
1 tsp. vanilla

Preheat the oven to 350°F. In a medium bowl, cream butter, egg and vanilla. Add the Cowboy Cookie Mix. Stir until the mixture is well blended. You may need to use your hands to finish mixing. Shape dough into walnut sized balls. Place dough balls 2 inches apart on a greased cookie sheet. Bake for 11 to 13 minutes. Transfer to wire racks to cool.

Cowboy Cookies
Makes 2 1/2 to 3 dozen

1 jar Cowboy Cookie Mix
1/2 C. butter or margarine,
   melted

1 egg
1 tsp. vanilla

Preheat the oven to 350°F. In a medium bowl, cream butter, egg and vanilla. Add the Cowboy Cookie Mix. Stir until the mixture is well blended. You may need to use your hands to finish mixing. Shape dough into walnut sized balls. Place dough balls 2 inches apart on a greased cookie sheet. Bake for 11 to 13 minutes. Transfer to wire racks to cool.

Cowboy Cookies
Makes 2 1/2 to 3 dozen

1 jar Cowboy Cookie Mix
1/2 C. butter or margarine,
   melted

1 egg
1 tsp. vanilla

Preheat the oven to 350°F. In a medium bowl, cream butter, egg and vanilla. Add the Cowboy Cookie Mix. Stir until the mixture is well blended. You may need to use your hands to finish mixing. Shape dough into walnut sized balls. Place dough balls 2 inches apart on a greased cookie sheet. Bake for 11 to 13 minutes. Transfer to wire racks to cool.

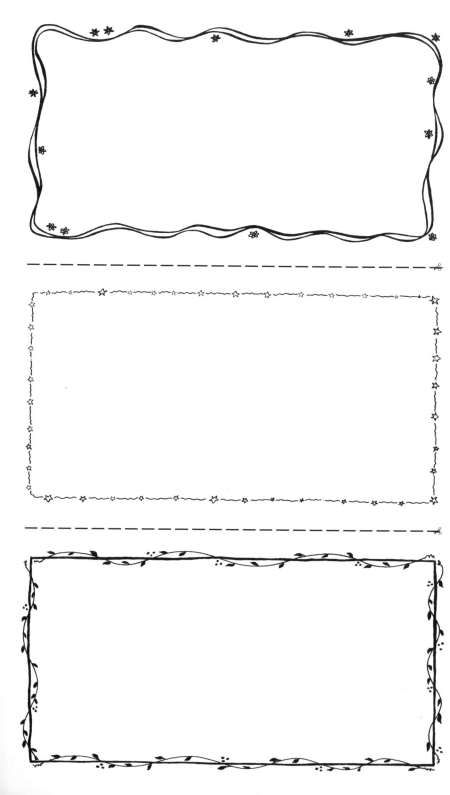

Chocolate Cookie Mix

3/4 C. dark brown sugar
1/2 C. sugar
1/4 C. unsweetened cocoa (clean inside of jar with a paper towel after this layer)
1/2 C. chopped pecans
1 C. semi-sweet chocolate chips
1 3/4 C. all-purpose flour
1 tsp. baking soda
1 tsp. baking powder
1/4 tsp. salt

Layer the ingredients in the order given into a wide-mouth 1-quart canning jar. Pack each layer in place before adding the next ingredient.

Attach a gift tag with the mixing and baking directions.

❀ A half-yard of fabric should make eight wide-mouth jar covers. ❀

Chocolate Cookies

Makes 2 to 3 dozen

1 jar Chocolate Cookie Mix
3/4 C. butter or margarine,
   softened
1 egg
1 tsp. vanilla

Preheat the oven to 350°F. In a large bowl, cream butter, egg and vanilla. Add the Chocolate Cookie Mix. Stir until the mixture is well blended. You may have to use your hands to finish mixing. Shape the dough into walnut size balls and place 2 inches apart on a greased cookie sheet. Bake for 11 to 13 minutes. Transfer to wire racks to cool.

Chocolate Cookies
Makes 2 to 3 dozen

1 jar Chocolate Cookie Mix
3/4 C. butter or margarine, softened

1 egg
1 tsp. vanilla

Preheat the oven to 350°F. In a large bowl, cream butter, egg and vanilla. Add the Chocolate Cookie Mix. Stir until the mixture is well blended. You may have to use your hands to finish mixing. Shape the dough into walnut size balls and place 2 inches apart on a greased cookie sheet. Bake for 11 to 13 minutes. Transfer to wire racks to cool.

Chocolate Cookies
Makes 2 to 3 dozen

1 jar Chocolate Cookie Mix
3/4 C. butter or margarine, softened

1 egg
1 tsp. vanilla

Preheat the oven to 350°F. In a large bowl, cream butter, egg and vanilla. Add the Chocolate Cookie Mix. Stir until the mixture is well blended. You may have to use your hands to finish mixing. Shape the dough into walnut size balls and place 2 inches apart on a greased cookie sheet. Bake for 11 to 13 minutes. Transfer to wire racks to cool.

Chocolate Cookies
Makes 2 to 3 dozen

1 jar Chocolate Cookie Mix
3/4 C. butter or margarine, softened

1 egg
1 tsp. vanilla

Preheat the oven to 350°F. In a large bowl, cream butter, egg and vanilla. Add the Chocolate Cookie Mix. Stir until the mixture is well blended. You may have to use your hands to finish mixing. Shape the dough into walnut size balls and place 2 inches apart on a greased cookie sheet. Bake for 11 to 13 minutes. Transfer to wire racks to cool.

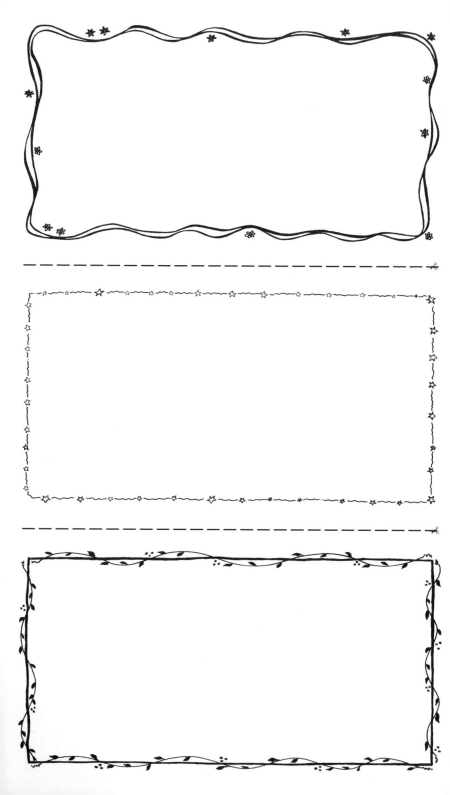

Chocolate Cookies
Makes 2 to 3 dozen

1 jar Chocolate Cookie Mix
3/4 C. butter or margarine,
softened

1 egg
1 tsp. vanilla

Preheat the oven to 350°F. In a large bowl, cream butter, egg and vanilla. Add the Chocolate Cookie Mix. Stir until the mixture is well blended. You may have to use your hands to finish mixing. Shape the dough into walnut size balls and place 2 inches apart on a greased cookie sheet. Bake for 11 to 13 minutes. Transfer to wire racks to cool.

Chocolate Cookies
Makes 2 to 3 dozen

1 jar Chocolate Cookie Mix
3/4 C. butter or margarine,
softened

1 egg
1 tsp. vanilla

Preheat the oven to 350°F. In a large bowl, cream butter, egg and vanilla. Add the Chocolate Cookie Mix. Stir until the mixture is well blended. You may have to use your hands to finish mixing. Shape the dough into walnut size balls and place 2 inches apart on a greased cookie sheet. Bake for 11 to 13 minutes. Transfer to wire racks to cool.

Chocolate Cookies
Makes 2 to 3 dozen

1 jar Chocolate Cookie Mix
3/4 C. butter or margarine,
softened

1 egg
1 tsp. vanilla

Preheat the oven to 350°F. In a large bowl, cream butter, egg and vanilla. Add the Chocolate Cookie Mix. Stir until the mixture is well blended. You may have to use your hands to finish mixing. Shape the dough into walnut size balls and place 2 inches apart on a greased cookie sheet. Bake for 11 to 13 minutes. Transfer to wire racks to cool.

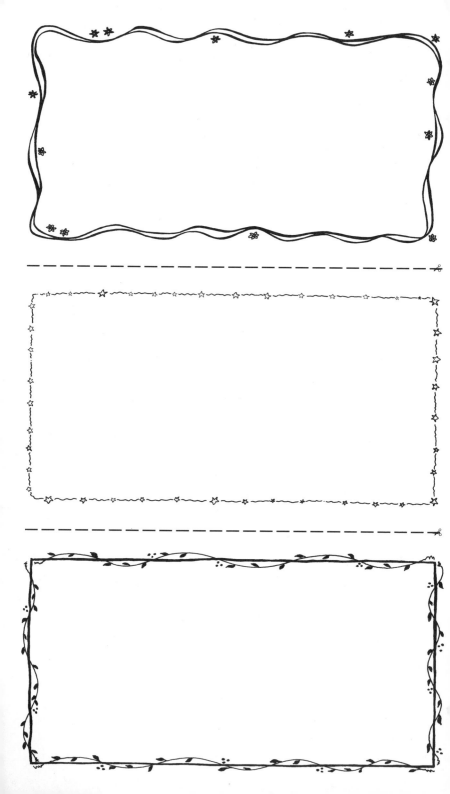

Sand Art Cookie Mix

      1/2 C. sugar
      1/2 C. old-fashioned oats
      1/2 C. M&M's
      1/2 C. brown sugar
      1 1/4 C. all-purpose flour
      1/2 tsp. baking powder
      1/2 tsp. salt
      1/2 C. crisp rice cereal
      1/2 C. semi-sweet chocolate
        chips

Layer the ingredients in the order given into a wide-mouth 1-quart canning jar. Pack each layer in place before adding the next ingredient.

Attach a gift tag with the mixing and baking directions.

Sand Art Cookies

Makes 1 1/2 to 2 dozen

1 jar Sand Art Cookie Mix
1/2 C. butter or margarine,
  melted
1 egg

Preheat the oven to 350°F. In a large bowl, cream the butter and egg. Add the Sand Art Cookie Mix. Stir until the mixture is well blended. Form dough into 1-inch balls and place 2 inches apart on a greased cookie sheet. Bake for 10 to 12 minutes. Transfer to wire racks to cool.

Sand Art Cookies
Makes 1 1/2 to 2 dozen

1 jar Sand Art Cookie Mix   1 egg
1/2 C. butter or margarine,
   melted

Preheat the oven to 350°F. In a large bowl, cream the butter and egg. Add the Sand Art Cookie Mix. Stir until the mixture is well blended. Form dough into 1-inch balls and place 2 inches apart on a greased cookie sheet. Bake for 10 to 12 minutes. Transfer to wire racks to cool.

Sand Art Cookies
Makes 1 1/2 to 2 dozen

1 jar Sand Art Cookie Mix   1 egg
1/2 C. butter or margarine,
   melted

Preheat the oven to 350°F. In a large bowl, cream the butter and egg. Add the Sand Art Cookie Mix. Stir until the mixture is well blended. Form dough into 1-inch balls and place 2 inches apart on a greased cookie sheet. Bake for 10 to 12 minutes. Transfer to wire racks to cool.

Sand Art Cookies
Makes 1 1/2 to 2 dozen

1 jar Sand Art Cookie Mix   1 egg
1/2 C. butter or margarine,
   melted

Preheat the oven to 350°F. In a large bowl, cream the butter and egg. Add the Sand Art Cookie Mix. Stir until the mixture is well blended. Form dough into 1-inch balls and place 2 inches apart on a greased cookie sheet. Bake for 10 to 12 minutes. Transfer to wire racks to cool.

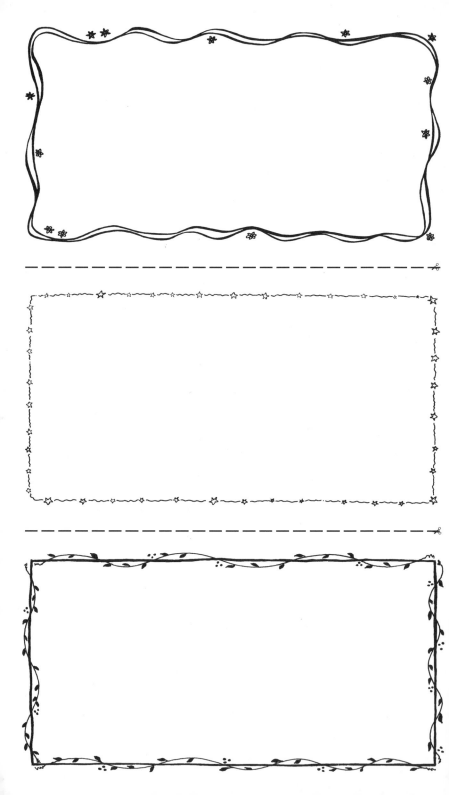

Sand Art Cookies
Makes 1 1/2 to 2 dozen

1 jar Sand Art Cookie Mix   1 egg
1/2 C. butter or margarine,
  melted

    Preheat the oven to 350°F. In a large bowl, cream the butter and egg. Add the Sand Art Cookie Mix. Stir until the mixture is well blended. Form dough into 1-inch balls and place 2 inches apart on a greased cookie sheet. Bake for 10 to 12 minutes. Transfer to wire racks to cool.

Sand Art Cookies
Makes 1 1/2 to 2 dozen

1 jar Sand Art Cookie Mix   1 egg
1/2 C. butter or margarine,
  melted

    Preheat the oven to 350°F. In a large bowl, cream the butter and egg. Add the Sand Art Cookie Mix. Stir until the mixture is well blended. Form dough into 1-inch balls and place 2 inches apart on a greased cookie sheet. Bake for 10 to 12 minutes. Transfer to wire racks to cool.

Sand Art Cookies
Makes 1 1/2 to 2 dozen

1 jar Sand Art Cookie Mix   1 egg
1/2 C. butter or margarine,
  melted

    Preheat the oven to 350°F. In a large bowl, cream the butter and egg. Add the Sand Art Cookie Mix. Stir until the mixture is well blended. Form dough into 1-inch balls and place 2 inches apart on a greased cookie sheet. Bake for 10 to 12 minutes. Transfer to wire racks to cool.

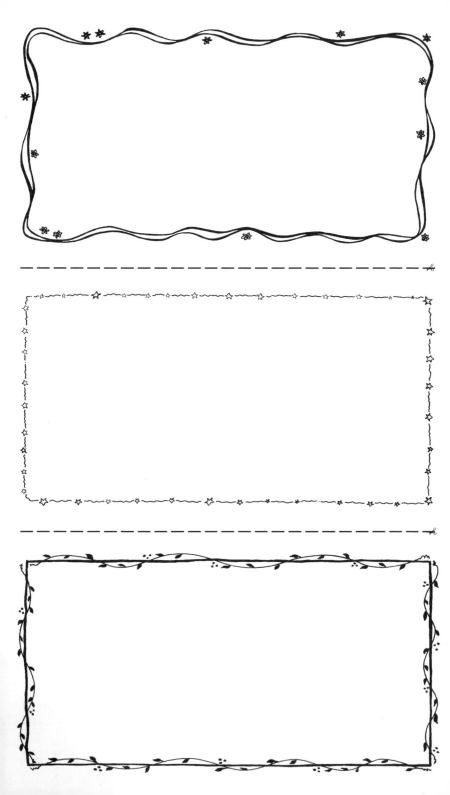

Potato Chip Cookie Mix

1 C. sugar
1/2 C. chopped pecans
1 1/2 C. crushed potato chips
2 1/2 C. all-purpose flour
1 tsp. baking powder

Layer the ingredients in the order given into a wide-mouth 1-quart canning jar. Pack each layer in place before adding the next ingredient.

Attach a gift tag with the mixing and baking directions.

Potato Chip Cookies

Makes 2 to 2 1/2 dozen

1 jar Potato Chip Cookie Mix
1 C. butter or margarine,
    softened
1 egg
1 tsp. vanilla

Preheat the oven to 350°F. In a large bowl, cream the butter, egg and vanilla. Add the Potato Chip Cookie Mix. Stir until the mixture is well blended. Shape the dough into walnut size balls. Place dough balls 2 inches apart on a greased cookie sheet and flatten. Bake for 14 to 18 minutes or until edges are very lightly browned. Transfer to wire racks to cool.

Potato Chip Cookies
Makes 2 to 2 1/2 dozen

1 jar Potato Chip Cookie Mix
1 C. butter or margarine,
   softened

1 egg
1 tsp. vanilla

Preheat the oven to 350°F. In a large bowl, cream the butter, egg and vanilla. Add the Potato Chip Cookie Mix. Stir until the mixture is well blended. Shape the dough into walnut size balls. Place dough balls 2 inches apart on a greased cookie sheet and flatten. Bake for 14 to 18 minutes or until edges are very lightly browned. Transfer to wire racks to cool.

Potato Chip Cookies
Makes 2 to 2 1/2 dozen

1 jar Potato Chip Cookie Mix
1 C. butter or margarine,
   softened

1 egg
1 tsp. vanilla

Preheat the oven to 350°F. In a large bowl, cream the butter, egg and vanilla. Add the Potato Chip Cookie Mix. Stir until the mixture is well blended. Shape the dough into walnut size balls. Place dough balls 2 inches apart on a greased cookie sheet and flatten. Bake for 14 to 18 minutes or until edges are very lightly browned. Transfer to wire racks to cool.

Potato Chip Cookies
Makes 2 to 2 1/2 dozen

1 jar Potato Chip Cookie Mix
1 C. butter or margarine,
   softened

1 egg
1 tsp. vanilla

Preheat the oven to 350°F. In a large bowl, cream the butter, egg and vanilla. Add the Potato Chip Cookie Mix. Stir until the mixture is well blended. Shape the dough into walnut size balls. Place dough balls 2 inches apart on a greased cookie sheet and flatten. Bake for 14 to 18 minutes or until edges are very lightly browned. Transfer to wire racks to cool.

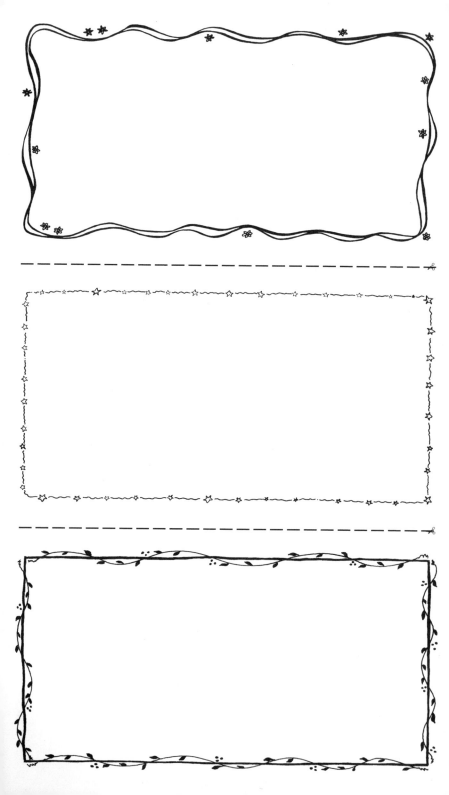

Potato Chip Cookies
Makes 2 to 2 1/2 dozen

1 jar Potato Chip Cookie Mix
1 C. butter or margarine, softened

1 egg
1 tsp. vanilla

Preheat the oven to 350°F. In a large bowl, cream the butter, egg and vanilla. Add the Potato Chip Cookie Mix. Stir until the mixture is well blended. Shape the dough into walnut size balls. Place dough balls 2 inches apart on a greased cookie sheet and flatten. Bake for 14 to 18 minutes or until edges are very lightly browned. Transfer to wire racks to cool.

Potato Chip Cookies
Makes 2 to 2 1/2 dozen

1 jar Potato Chip Cookie Mix
1 C. butter or margarine, softened

1 egg
1 tsp. vanilla

Preheat the oven to 350°F. In a large bowl, cream the butter, egg and vanilla. Add the Potato Chip Cookie Mix. Stir until the mixture is well blended. Shape the dough into walnut size balls. Place dough balls 2 inches apart on a greased cookie sheet and flatten. Bake for 14 to 18 minutes or until edges are very lightly browned. Transfer to wire racks to cool.

Potato Chip Cookies
Makes 2 to 2 1/2 dozen

1 jar Potato Chip Cookie Mix
1 C. butter or margarine, softened

1 egg
1 tsp. vanilla

Preheat the oven to 350°F. In a large bowl, cream the butter, egg and vanilla. Add the Potato Chip Cookie Mix. Stir until the mixture is well blended. Shape the dough into walnut size balls. Place dough balls 2 inches apart on a greased cookie sheet and flatten. Bake for 14 to 18 minutes or until edges are very lightly browned. Transfer to wire racks to cool.

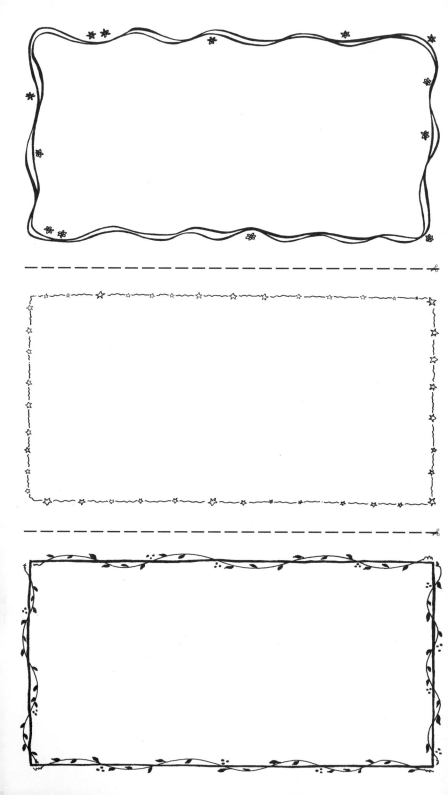

Munchy Crunchy Cookie Mix

1 C. all-purpose flour
1/2 tsp. baking powder
3/4 tsp. baking soda
1/4 tsp. salt
1/2 C. sugar
3/4 C. brown sugar
1/2 C. cornflakes cereal
2 T. flaked coconut
1/2 C. semi-sweet chocolate
  chips
1 C. old-fashioned oats

Layer the ingredients in the order given into a wide-mouth 1-quart canning jar. Pack each layer in place before adding the next ingredient.

Attach a gift tag with the mixing and baking directions.

Munchy Crunchy Cookies

Makes 2 to 3 dozen

1 jar Munchy Crunchy Cookie Mix
1/2 C. butter or margarine,
  melted
1 egg
1/4 tsp. vanilla

Preheat the oven to 350°F. In a large bowl, cream butter, egg and vanilla. Add the Munchy Crunchy Cookie Mix. Stir until the mixture is well blended. Shape dough into 2-inch balls and place on an ungreased cookie sheet. Bake for 10 to 12 minutes. Transfer to wire racks to cool.

Munchy Crunchy Cookies
Makes 2 to 3 dozen

1 jar Munchy Crunchy
   Cookie Mix
1/2 C. butter or margarine,
   melted

1 egg
1/4 tsp. vanilla

     Preheat the oven to 350°F. In a large bowl, cream butter, egg and vanilla. Add the Munchy Crunchy Cookie Mix. Stir until the mixture is well blended. Shape dough into 2-inch balls and place on an ungreased cookie sheet. Bake for 10 to 12 minutes. Transfer to wire racks to cool.

Munchy Crunchy Cookies
Makes 2 to 3 dozen

1 jar Munchy Crunchy
   Cookie Mix
1/2 C. butter or margarine,
   melted

1 egg
1/4 tsp. vanilla

     Preheat the oven to 350°F. In a large bowl, cream butter, egg and vanilla. Add the Munchy Crunchy Cookie Mix. Stir until the mixture is well blended. Shape dough into 2-inch balls and place on an ungreased cookie sheet. Bake for 10 to 12 minutes. Transfer to wire racks to cool.

Munchy Crunchy Cookies
Makes 2 to 3 dozen

1 jar Munchy Crunchy
   Cookie Mix
1/2 C. butter or margarine,
   melted

1 egg
1/4 tsp. vanilla

     Preheat the oven to 350°F. In a large bowl, cream butter, egg and vanilla. Add the Munchy Crunchy Cookie Mix. Stir until the mixture is well blended. Shape dough into 2-inch balls and place on an ungreased cookie sheet. Bake for 10 to 12 minutes. Transfer to wire racks to cool.

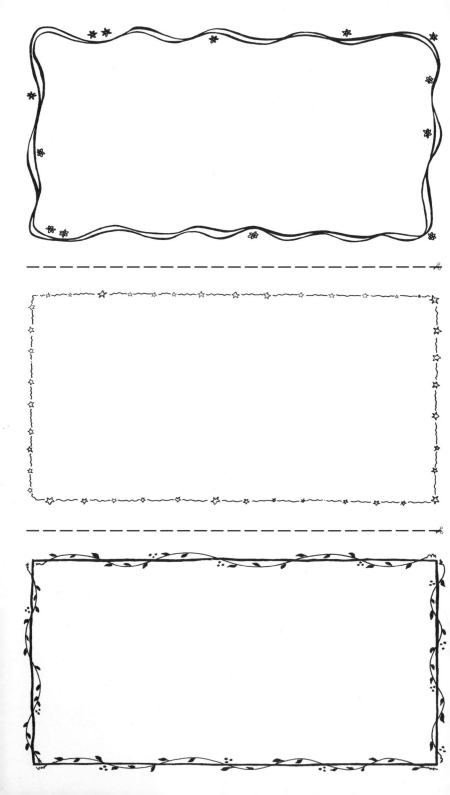

Munchy Crunchy Cookies
Makes 2 to 3 dozen

1 jar Munchy Crunchy
  Cookie Mix
1/2 C. butter or margarine,
  melted

1 egg
1/4 tsp. vanilla

Preheat the oven to 350°F. In a large bowl, cream butter, egg and vanilla. Add the Munchy Crunchy Cookie Mix. Stir until the mixture is well blended. Shape dough into 2-inch balls and place on an ungreased cookie sheet. Bake for 10 to 12 minutes. Transfer to wire racks to cool.

Munchy Crunchy Cookies
Makes 2 to 3 dozen

1 jar Munchy Crunchy
  Cookie Mix
1/2 C. butter or margarine,
  melted

1 egg
1/4 tsp. vanilla

Preheat the oven to 350°F. In a large bowl, cream butter, egg and vanilla. Add the Munchy Crunchy Cookie Mix. Stir until the mixture is well blended. Shape dough into 2-inch balls and place on an ungreased cookie sheet. Bake for 10 to 12 minutes. Transfer to wire racks to cool.

Munchy Crunchy Cookies
Makes 2 to 3 dozen

1 jar Munchy Crunchy
  Cookie Mix
1/2 C. butter or margarine,
  melted

1 egg
1/4 tsp. vanilla

Preheat the oven to 350°F. In a large bowl, cream butter, egg and vanilla. Add the Munchy Crunchy Cookie Mix. Stir until the mixture is well blended. Shape dough into 2-inch balls and place on an ungreased cookie sheet. Bake for 10 to 12 minutes. Transfer to wire racks to cool.

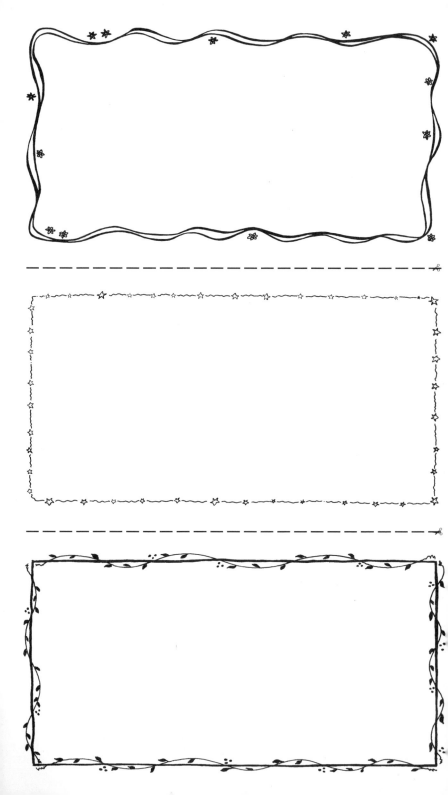

Celebration Cookie Mix

1 C. quick rolled oats
1/2 tsp. cinnamon
1/3 C. chopped walnuts
1 C. mini M&M's
1/3 C. raisins
3/4 C. brown sugar
3/4 C. all-purpose flour
1/2 tsp. baking soda
1/2 tsp. salt

Layer the ingredients in the order given into a wide-mouth 1-quart canning jar. Pack each layer in place before adding the next ingredient.

Attach a gift tag with the mixing and baking directions.

Celebration Cookies

Makes 3 to 4 dozen

1 jar Celebration Cookie Mix
3/4 C. butter or margarine,
   softened
1 egg
3/4 tsp. vanilla

Preheat the oven to 350°F. In a large bowl, cream the butter, egg and vanilla. Add the Celebration Cookie Mix. Stir until the mixture is well blended. Shape into 1-inch balls and place about 2 inches apart on greased cookie sheets. Bake for 12 to 15 minutes. Transfer to wire racks to cool.

Celebration Cookies

Makes 3 to 4 dozen

1 jar Celebration Cookie Mix
3/4 C. butter or margarine,
 softened

1 egg
3/4 tsp. vanilla

Preheat the oven to 350°F. In a large bowl, cream the butter, egg and vanilla. Add the Celebration Cookie Mix. Stir until the mixture is well blended. Shape into 1-inch balls and place about 2 inches apart on greased cookie sheets. Bake for 12 to 15 minutes. Transfer to wire racks to cool.

Celebration Cookies

Makes 3 to 4 dozen

1 jar Celebration Cookie Mix
3/4 C. butter or margarine,
 softened

1 egg
3/4 tsp. vanilla

Preheat the oven to 350°F. In a large bowl, cream the butter, egg and vanilla. Add the Celebration Cookie Mix. Stir until the mixture is well blended. Shape into 1-inch balls and place about 2 inches apart on greased cookie sheets. Bake for 12 to 15 minutes. Transfer to wire racks to cool.

Celebration Cookies

Makes 3 to 4 dozen

1 jar Celebration Cookie Mix
3/4 C. butter or margarine,
 softened

1 egg
3/4 tsp. vanilla

Preheat the oven to 350°F. In a large bowl, cream the butter, egg and vanilla. Add the Celebration Cookie Mix. Stir until the mixture is well blended. Shape into 1-inch balls and place about 2 inches apart on greased cookie sheets. Bake for 12 to 15 minutes. Transfer to wire racks to cool.

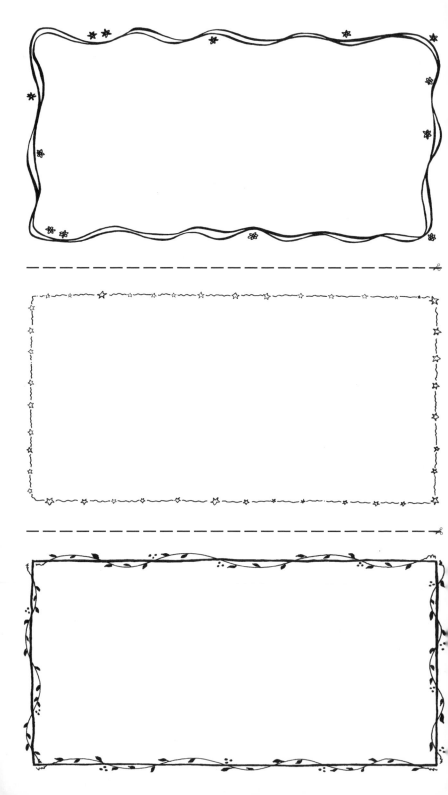

Celebration Cookies
Makes 3 to 4 dozen

1 jar Celebration Cookie Mix
3/4 C. butter or margarine,
softened

1 egg
3/4 tsp. vanilla

Preheat the oven to 350°F. In a large bowl, cream the butter, egg and vanilla. Add the Celebration Cookie Mix. Stir until the mixture is well blended. Shape into 1-inch balls and place about 2 inches apart on greased cookie sheets. Bake for 12 to 15 minutes. Transfer to wire racks to cool.

Celebration Cookies
Makes 3 to 4 dozen

1 jar Celebration Cookie Mix
3/4 C. butter or margarine,
softened

1 egg
3/4 tsp. vanilla

Preheat the oven to 350°F. In a large bowl, cream the butter, egg and vanilla. Add the Celebration Cookie Mix. Stir until the mixture is well blended. Shape into 1-inch balls and place about 2 inches apart on greased cookie sheets. Bake for 12 to 15 minutes. Transfer to wire racks to cool.

Celebration Cookies
Makes 3 to 4 dozen

1 jar Celebration Cookie Mix
3/4 C. butter or margarine,
softened

1 egg
3/4 tsp. vanilla

Preheat the oven to 350°F. In a large bowl, cream the butter, egg and vanilla. Add the Celebration Cookie Mix. Stir until the mixture is well blended. Shape into 1-inch balls and place about 2 inches apart on greased cookie sheets. Bake for 12 to 15 minutes. Transfer to wire racks to cool.

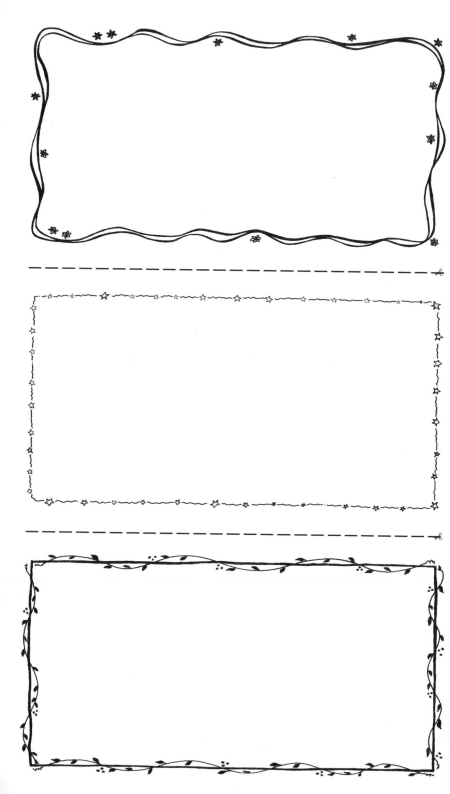

Chocolate Chip Muffin Delights Mix

1/2 C. brown sugar
1 1/2 C. finely crushed graham
    cracker crumbs
1 C. mini chocolate chips
1 C. crushed walnuts or pecans

    Layer the ingredients in the order given into a wide-mouth 1-quart canning jar. Pack each layer in place before adding the next ingredient.

    Attach a gift tag with the mixing and baking directions.

Pick a theme and add anything you want to help decorate the jar.

Chocolate Chip Muffin Delights

Makes 2 to 3 dozen

1 jar Chocolate Chip Muffin
   Delights Mix
1/2 C. evaporated milk
1/4 C. butter or margarine,
   melted

Preheat the oven to 375°F. In a large bowl, mix evaporated milk and butter. Add the Chocolate Chip Muffin Delights Mix. Stir until the mixture is well blended. Pour into a greased mini muffin pan. Bake for 10 to 12 minutes. Transfer to wire racks to cool.

Chocolate Chip Muffin Delights

Makes 2 to 3 dozen

1 jar Chocolate Chip Muffin
   Delights Mix
1/2 C. evaporated milk

1/4 C. butter or margarine,
   melted

Preheat the oven to 375°F. In a large bowl, mix evaporated milk and butter. Add the Chocolate Chip Muffin Delights Mix. Stir until the mixture is well blended. Pour into a greased mini muffin pan. Bake for 10 to 12 minutes. Transfer to wire racks to cool.

Chocolate Chip Muffin Delights

Makes 2 to 3 dozen

1 jar Chocolate Chip Muffin
   Delights Mix
1/2 C. evaporated milk

1/4 C. butter or margarine,
   melted

Preheat the oven to 375°F. In a large bowl, mix evaporated milk and butter. Add the Chocolate Chip Muffin Delights Mix. Stir until the mixture is well blended. Pour into a greased mini muffin pan. Bake for 10 to 12 minutes. Transfer to wire racks to cool.

Chocolate Chip Muffin Delights

Makes 2 to 3 dozen

1 jar Chocolate Chip Muffin
   Delights Mix
1/2 C. evaporated milk

1/4 C. butter or margarine,
   melted

Preheat the oven to 375°F. In a large bowl, mix evaporated milk and butter. Add the Chocolate Chip Muffin Delights Mix. Stir until the mixture is well blended. Pour into a greased mini muffin pan. Bake for 10 to 12 minutes. Transfer to wire racks to cool.

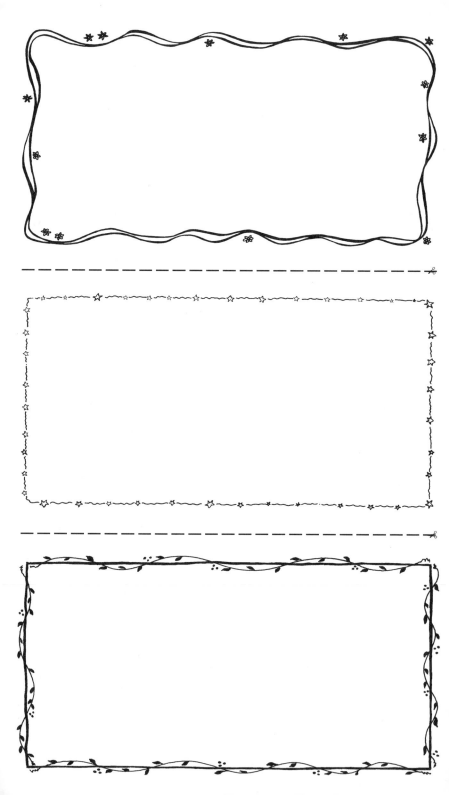

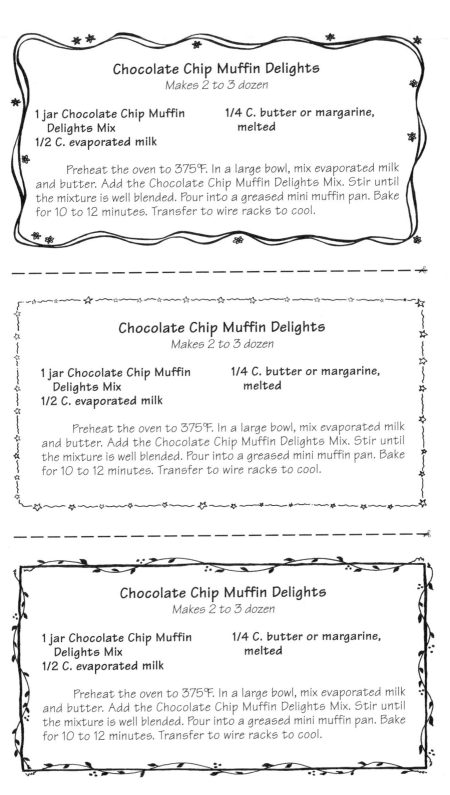

Chocolate Chip Muffin Delights
Makes 2 to 3 dozen

1 jar Chocolate Chip Muffin
   Delights Mix
1/2 C. evaporated milk

1/4 C. butter or margarine,
   melted

    Preheat the oven to 375°F. In a large bowl, mix evaporated milk and butter. Add the Chocolate Chip Muffin Delights Mix. Stir until the mixture is well blended. Pour into a greased mini muffin pan. Bake for 10 to 12 minutes. Transfer to wire racks to cool.

Chocolate Chip Muffin Delights
Makes 2 to 3 dozen

1 jar Chocolate Chip Muffin
   Delights Mix
1/2 C. evaporated milk

1/4 C. butter or margarine,
   melted

    Preheat the oven to 375°F. In a large bowl, mix evaporated milk and butter. Add the Chocolate Chip Muffin Delights Mix. Stir until the mixture is well blended. Pour into a greased mini muffin pan. Bake for 10 to 12 minutes. Transfer to wire racks to cool.

Chocolate Chip Muffin Delights
Makes 2 to 3 dozen

1 jar Chocolate Chip Muffin
   Delights Mix
1/2 C. evaporated milk

1/4 C. butter or margarine,
   melted

    Preheat the oven to 375°F. In a large bowl, mix evaporated milk and butter. Add the Chocolate Chip Muffin Delights Mix. Stir until the mixture is well blended. Pour into a greased mini muffin pan. Bake for 10 to 12 minutes. Transfer to wire racks to cool.

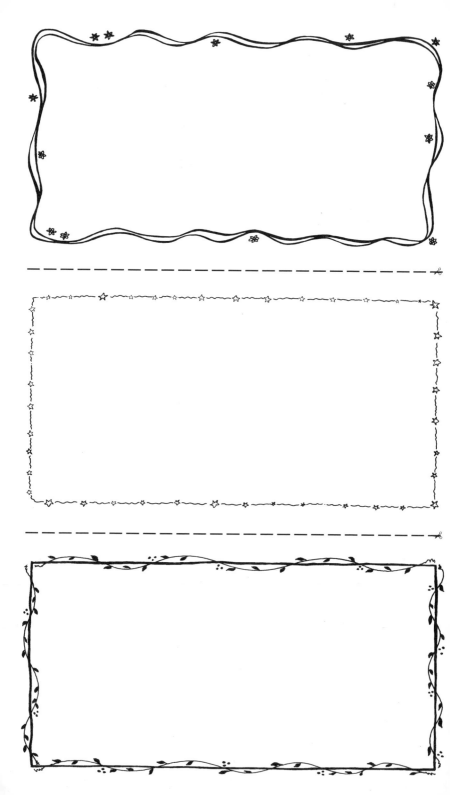

Magic Cookie Bar Mix

3/4 C. chocolate chips
1 1/3 C. flaked coconut
1 C. coarsely chopped pecans
1 1/2 C. graham cracker
   crumbs, placed in a baggie or
   wrapped in plastic wrap

Layer the ingredients in the order given into a wide-mouth 1-quart canning jar. Pack each layer in place before adding the next ingredient.

Attach a gift tag with the mixing and baking directions.

❋ For an out of the ordinary gift, try placing the mix in a mixing bowl along with kitchen utensils, cookbooks, recipe cards, towels and pot holders. ❋

Magic Cookie Bars

1 jar Magic Cookie Bar Mix
1/2 C. butter or margarine,
  melted
1 (14 oz.) can condensed milk

Preheat the oven to 350°F (325°F for glass dish). In a 9 x 12 inch baking pan, melt butter in the oven. Remove cracker crumbs from jar and sprinkle over the butter. Pour the condensed milk evenly over the crumbs. Top evenly with the remaining Magic Cookie Bar Mix and press down firmly. Bake for 25 to 30 minutes or until the bars are lightly browned.

Magic Cookie Bars

1 jar Magic Cookie Bar Mix
1/2 C. butter or margarine,
  melted

1 (14 oz.) can condensed milk

Preheat the oven to 350°F (325°F for glass dish). In a 9 x 12 inch baking pan, melt butter in the oven. Remove cracker crumbs from jar and sprinkle over the butter. Pour the condensed milk evenly over the crumbs. Top evenly with the remaining Magic Cookie Bar Mix and press down firmly. Bake for 25 to 30 minutes or until the bars are lightly browned.

Magic Cookie Bars

1 jar Magic Cookie Bar Mix
1/2 C. butter or margarine,
  melted

1 (14 oz.) can condensed milk

Preheat the oven to 350°F (325°F for glass dish). In a 9 x 12 inch baking pan, melt butter in the oven. Remove cracker crumbs from jar and sprinkle over the butter. Pour the condensed milk evenly over the crumbs. Top evenly with the remaining Magic Cookie Bar Mix and press down firmly. Bake for 25 to 30 minutes or until the bars are lightly browned.

Magic Cookie Bars

1 jar Magic Cookie Bar Mix
1/2 C. butter or margarine,
  melted

1 (14 oz.) can condensed milk

Preheat the oven to 350°F (325°F for glass dish). In a 9 x 12 inch baking pan, melt butter in the oven. Remove cracker crumbs from jar and sprinkle over the butter. Pour the condensed milk evenly over the crumbs. Top evenly with the remaining Magic Cookie Bar Mix and press down firmly. Bake for 25 to 30 minutes or until the bars are lightly browned.

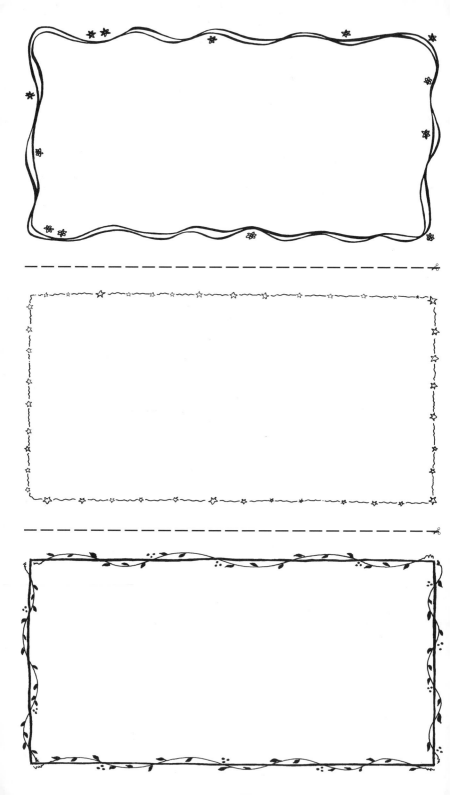

Magic Cookie Bars

1 jar Magic Cookie Bar Mix
1/2 C. butter or margarine,
   melted

1 (14 oz.) can condensed milk

Preheat the oven to 350°F (325°F for glass dish). In a 9 x 12 inch baking pan, melt butter in the oven. Remove cracker crumbs from jar and sprinkle over the butter. Pour the condensed milk evenly over the crumbs. Top evenly with the remaining Magic Cookie Bar Mix and press down firmly. Bake for 25 to 30 minutes or until the bars are lightly browned.

Magic Cookie Bars

1 jar Magic Cookie Bar Mix
1/2 C. butter or margarine,
   melted

1 (14 oz.) can condensed milk

Preheat the oven to 350°F (325°F for glass dish). In a 9 x 12 inch baking pan, melt butter in the oven. Remove cracker crumbs from jar and sprinkle over the butter. Pour the condensed milk evenly over the crumbs. Top evenly with the remaining Magic Cookie Bar Mix and press down firmly. Bake for 25 to 30 minutes or until the bars are lightly browned.

Magic Cookie Bars

1 jar Magic Cookie Bar Mix
1/2 C. butter or margarine,
   melted

1 (14 oz.) can condensed milk

Preheat the oven to 350°F (325°F for glass dish). In a 9 x 12 inch baking pan, melt butter in the oven. Remove cracker crumbs from jar and sprinkle over the butter. Pour the condensed milk evenly over the crumbs. Top evenly with the remaining Magic Cookie Bar Mix and press down firmly. Bake for 25 to 30 minutes or until the bars are lightly browned.

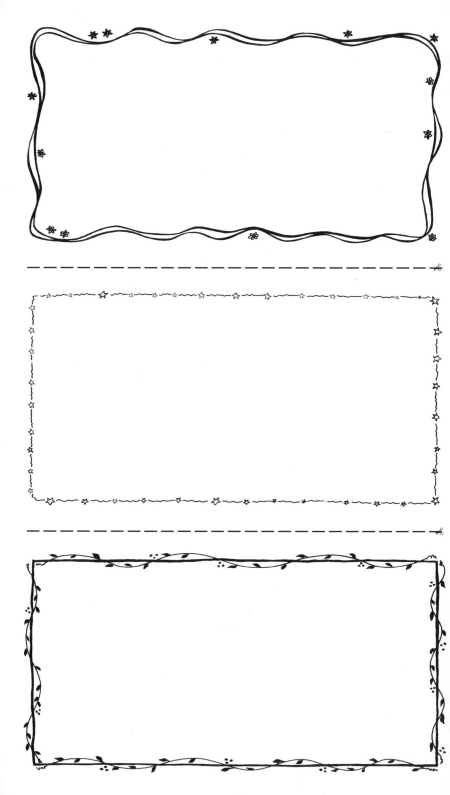

Treasure Chest Cookie Mix

2 C. old-fashioned oats
1 C. brown sugar
1/2 C. mini M&M's
1/3 C. sugar
1/2 tsp. baking soda
1/4 tsp. salt
1/2 C. mini chocolate chips

Layer the ingredients in the order given into a wide-mouth 1-quart canning jar. Pack each layer in place before adding the next ingredient.

Attach a gift tag with the mixing and baking directions.

❋ *For a different look, place a small amount of stuffing under a fabric cover before attaching to "puff" the top.* ❋

Treasure Chest Cookies

Makes 3 to 4 dozen

1 jar Treasure Chest Cookie Mix
1/4 C. butter or margarine,
   softened
1/2 C. peanut butter
1 egg
1/2 tsp. vanilla

Preheat the oven to 375°F. In a large bowl, cream the butter, peanut butter, egg and vanilla. Slowly add and stir the Treasure Chest Cookie Mix until the mixture is well blended. Form dough into 1-inch balls and place on a greased cookie sheet. Dip the bottom of a glass in sugar and use to flatten cookies. Bake for 11 to 12 minutes. Transfer to wire racks to cool.

Treasure Chest Cookies
Makes 3 to 4 dozen

1 jar Treasure Chest Cookie Mix
1/4 C. butter or margarine,
    softened

1/2 C. peanut butter
1 egg
1/2 tsp. vanilla

Preheat the oven to 375°F. In a large bowl, cream the butter, peanut butter, egg and vanilla. Slowly add and stir the Treasure Chest Cookie Mix until the mixture is well blended. Form dough into 1-inch balls and place on a greased cookie sheet. Dip the bottom of a glass in sugar and use to flatten cookies. Bake for 11 to 12 minutes. Transfer to wire racks to cool.

Treasure Chest Cookies
Makes 3 to 4 dozen

1 jar Treasure Chest Cookie Mix
1/4 C. butter or margarine,
    softened

1/2 C. peanut butter
1 egg
1/2 tsp. vanilla

Preheat the oven to 375°F. In a large bowl, cream the butter, peanut butter, egg and vanilla. Slowly add and stir the Treasure Chest Cookie Mix until the mixture is well blended. Form dough into 1-inch balls and place on a greased cookie sheet. Dip the bottom of a glass in sugar and use to flatten cookies. Bake for 11 to 12 minutes. Transfer to wire racks to cool.

Treasure Chest Cookies
Makes 3 to 4 dozen

1 jar Treasure Chest Cookie Mix
1/4 C. butter or margarine,
    softened

1/2 C. peanut butter
1 egg
1/2 tsp. vanilla

Preheat the oven to 375°F. In a large bowl, cream the butter, peanut butter, egg and vanilla. Slowly add and stir the Treasure Chest Cookie Mix until the mixture is well blended. Form dough into 1-inch balls and place on a greased cookie sheet. Dip the bottom of a glass in sugar and use to flatten cookies. Bake for 11 to 12 minutes. Transfer to wire racks to cool.

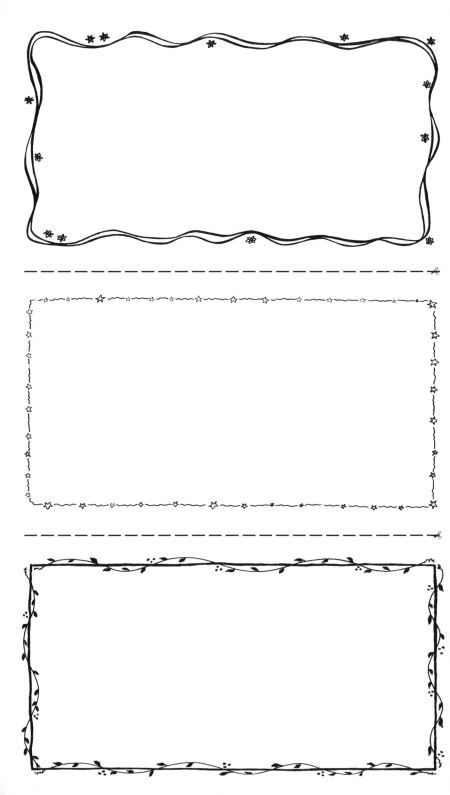

Treasure Chest Cookies
Makes 3 to 4 dozen

1 jar Treasure Chest Cookie Mix
1/4 C. butter or margarine,
  softened

1/2 C. peanut butter
1 egg
1/2 tsp. vanilla

Preheat the oven to 375°F. In a large bowl, cream the butter, peanut butter, egg and vanilla. Slowly add and stir the Treasure Chest Cookie Mix until the mixture is well blended. Form dough into 1-inch balls and place on a greased cookie sheet. Dip the bottom of a glass in sugar and use to flatten cookies. Bake for 11 to 12 minutes. Transfer to wire racks to cool.

Treasure Chest Cookies
Makes 3 to 4 dozen

1 jar Treasure Chest Cookie Mix
1/4 C. butter or margarine,
  softened

1/2 C. peanut butter
1 egg
1/2 tsp. vanilla

Preheat the oven to 375°F. In a large bowl, cream the butter, peanut butter, egg and vanilla. Slowly add and stir the Treasure Chest Cookie Mix until the mixture is well blended. Form dough into 1-inch balls and place on a greased cookie sheet. Dip the bottom of a glass in sugar and use to flatten cookies. Bake for 11 to 12 minutes. Transfer to wire racks to cool.

Treasure Chest Cookies
Makes 3 to 4 dozen

1 jar Treasure Chest Cookie Mix
1/4 C. butter or margarine,
  softened

1/2 C. peanut butter
1 egg
1/2 tsp. vanilla

Preheat the oven to 375°F. In a large bowl, cream the butter, peanut butter, egg and vanilla. Slowly add and stir the Treasure Chest Cookie Mix until the mixture is well blended. Form dough into 1-inch balls and place on a greased cookie sheet. Dip the bottom of a glass in sugar and use to flatten cookies. Bake for 11 to 12 minutes. Transfer to wire racks to cool.

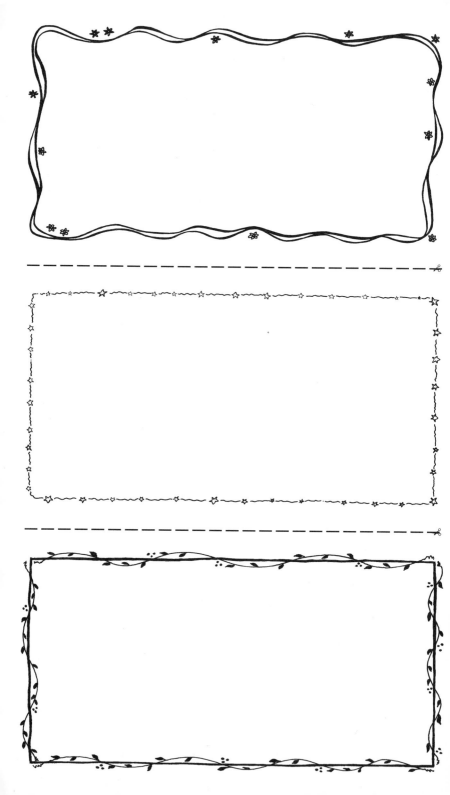

Almond Joy Brownie Mix

1 1/2 C. plus 3 T. sugar
6 T. unsweetened cocoa (clean
　　inside of jar with a paper towel
　　after this layer)
1 C. flaked coconut, sprinkled
　　with 1 tsp. almond extract and
　　tossed to blend
1/2 C. coarsely chopped almonds
1 C. flour
3/4 tsp. baking powder
3/4 tsp. salt

Layer the ingredients in the order given into a wide-mouth 1-quart canning jar. Pack each layer in place before adding the next ingredient.

Attach a gift tag with the mixing and baking directions.

Almond Joy Brownies

Makes 24 bars

1 jar Almond Joy Brownie Mix
9 T. butter or margarine, melted
3 eggs, slightly beaten

Preheat the oven to 350°F. In a large bowl, place Almond Joy Brownie Mix and stir until blended. Add butter and eggs and stir. Use your hands to thoroughly blend mixture. Spread batter in a greased 9 x 12 inch baking pan. Bake for 25 to 30 minutes. Cut brownies into 2-inch squares.

Almond Joy Brownies

Makes 24 bars

1 jar Almond Joy Brownie Mix
9 T. butter or margarine,
 melted

3 eggs, slightly beaten

Preheat the oven to 350°F. In a large bowl, place Almond Joy Brownie Mix and stir until blended. Add butter and eggs and stir. Use your hands to thoroughly blend mixture. Spread batter in a greased 9 x 12 inch baking pan. Bake for 25 to 30 minutes. Cut brownies into 2-inch squares.

Almond Joy Brownies

Makes 24 bars

1 jar Almond Joy Brownie Mix
9 T. butter or margarine,
 melted

3 eggs, slightly beaten

Preheat the oven to 350°F. In a large bowl, place Almond Joy Brownie Mix and stir until blended. Add butter and eggs and stir. Use your hands to thoroughly blend mixture. Spread batter in a greased 9 x 12 inch baking pan. Bake for 25 to 30 minutes. Cut brownies into 2-inch squares.

Almond Joy Brownies

Makes 24 bars

1 jar Almond Joy Brownie Mix
9 T. butter or margarine,
 melted

3 eggs, slightly beaten

Preheat the oven to 350°F. In a large bowl, place Almond Joy Brownie Mix and stir until blended. Add butter and eggs and stir. Use your hands to thoroughly blend mixture. Spread batter in a greased 9 x 12 inch baking pan. Bake for 25 to 30 minutes. Cut brownies into 2-inch squares.

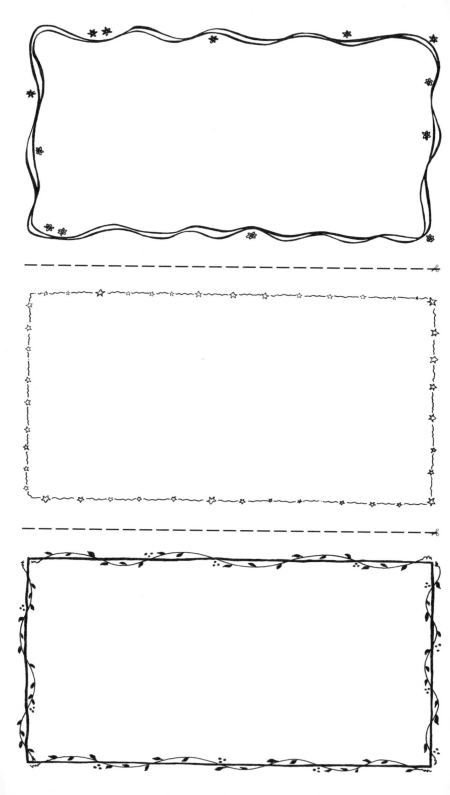

Almond Joy Brownies
Makes 24 bars

1 jar Almond Joy Brownie Mix
9 T. butter or margarine,
   melted

3 eggs, slightly beaten

Preheat the oven to 350°F. In a large bowl, place Almond Joy Brownie Mix and stir until blended. Add butter and eggs and stir. Use your hands to thoroughly blend mixture. Spread batter in a greased 9 x 12 inch baking pan. Bake for 25 to 30 minutes. Cut brownies into 2-inch squares.

Almond Joy Brownies
Makes 24 bars

1 jar Almond Joy Brownie Mix
9 T. butter or margarine,
   melted

3 eggs, slightly beaten

Preheat the oven to 350°F. In a large bowl, place Almond Joy Brownie Mix and stir until blended. Add butter and eggs and stir. Use your hands to thoroughly blend mixture. Spread batter in a greased 9 x 12 inch baking pan. Bake for 25 to 30 minutes. Cut brownies into 2-inch squares.

Almond Joy Brownies
Makes 24 bars

1 jar Almond Joy Brownie Mix
9 T. butter or margarine,
   melted

3 eggs, slightly beaten

Preheat the oven to 350°F. In a large bowl, place Almond Joy Brownie Mix and stir until blended. Add butter and eggs and stir. Use your hands to thoroughly blend mixture. Spread batter in a greased 9 x 12 inch baking pan. Bake for 25 to 30 minutes. Cut brownies into 2-inch squares.

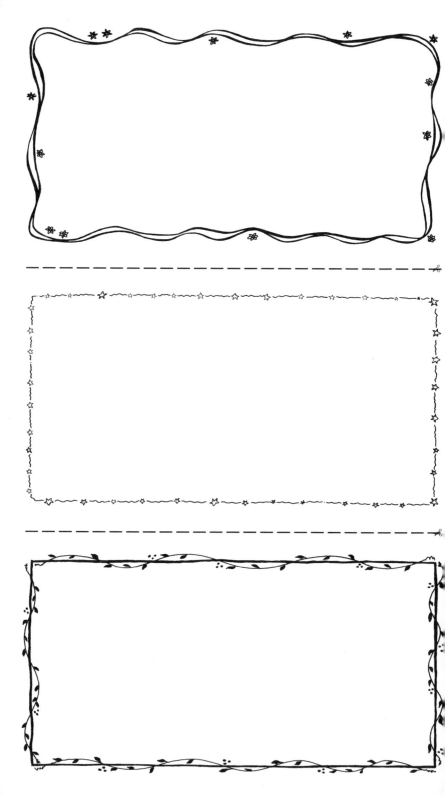

Ranger Cookie Mix

1 C. fruit flavored crisp rice cereal
1/3 C. flaked coconut
2/3 C. brown sugar
1 C. fruit flavored crisp rice cereal
1 1/4 C. all-purpose flour
1/2 tsp. baking powder
1/4 tsp. baking soda

Layer the ingredients in the order given into a wide-mouth 1-quart canning jar. Pack each layer in place before adding the next ingredient.

Attach a gift tag with the mixing and baking directions.

❀ At times, it may seem impossible to make all of the jar ingredients fit, but with persistence, they do all fit. ❀

Ranger Cookies

Makes 1 1/2 to 2 dozen

1 jar Ranger Cookie Mix
1/3 C. shortening
1 egg, slightly beaten
2 T. milk
1 tsp. vanilla

Preheat the oven to 375°F. In a large bowl, cream the shortening, egg, milk and vanilla. Add the Ranger Cookie Mix. Stir until the mixture is well blended. Drop by rounded teaspoonfuls 2 inches apart on an ungreased baking sheet. Bake for 8 to 9 minutes or until cookie edges are golden brown. Transfer to wire racks to cool.

Ranger Cookies
Makes 1 1/2 to 2 dozen

1 jar Ranger Cookie Mix
1/3 C. shortening
1 egg, slightly beaten

2 T. milk
1 tsp. vanilla

Preheat the oven to 375°F. In a large bowl, cream the shortening, egg, milk and vanilla. Add the Ranger Cookie Mix. Stir until the mixture is well blended. Drop by rounded teaspoonfuls 2 inches apart on an ungreased baking sheet. Bake for 8 to 9 minutes or until cookie edges are golden brown. Transfer to wire racks to cool.

Ranger Cookies
Makes 1 1/2 to 2 dozen

1 jar Ranger Cookie Mix
1/3 C. shortening
1 egg, slightly beaten

2 T. milk
1 tsp. vanilla

Preheat the oven to 375°F. In a large bowl, cream the shortening, egg, milk and vanilla. Add the Ranger Cookie Mix. Stir until the mixture is well blended. Drop by rounded teaspoonfuls 2 inches apart on an ungreased baking sheet. Bake for 8 to 9 minutes or until cookie edges are golden brown. Transfer to wire racks to cool.

Ranger Cookies
Makes 1 1/2 to 2 dozen

1 jar Ranger Cookie Mix
1/3 C. shortening
1 egg, slightly beaten

2 T. milk
1 tsp. vanilla

Preheat the oven to 375°F. In a large bowl, cream the shortening, egg, milk and vanilla. Add the Ranger Cookie Mix. Stir until the mixture is well blended. Drop by rounded teaspoonfuls 2 inches apart on an ungreased baking sheet. Bake for 8 to 9 minutes or until cookie edges are golden brown. Transfer to wire racks to cool.

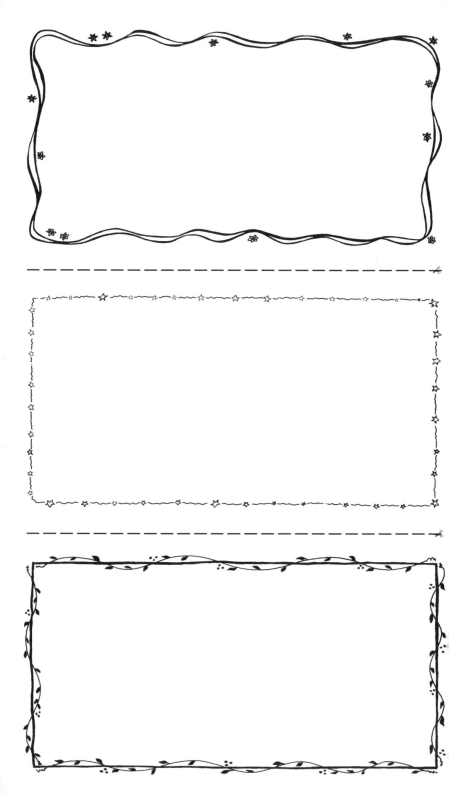

Ranger Cookies
Makes 1 1/2 to 2 dozen

1 jar Ranger Cookie Mix
1/3 C. shortening
1 egg, slightly beaten

2 T. milk
1 tsp. vanilla

Preheat the oven to 375°F. In a large bowl, cream the shortening, egg, milk and vanilla. Add the Ranger Cookie Mix. Stir until the mixture is well blended. Drop by rounded teaspoonfuls 2 inches apart on an ungreased baking sheet. Bake for 8 to 9 minutes or until cookie edges are golden brown. Transfer to wire racks to cool.

Ranger Cookies
Makes 1 1/2 to 2 dozen

1 jar Ranger Cookie Mix
1/3 C. shortening
1 egg, slightly beaten

2 T. milk
1 tsp. vanilla

Preheat the oven to 375°F. In a large bowl, cream the shortening, egg, milk and vanilla. Add the Ranger Cookie Mix. Stir until the mixture is well blended. Drop by rounded teaspoonfuls 2 inches apart on an ungreased baking sheet. Bake for 8 to 9 minutes or until cookie edges are golden brown. Transfer to wire racks to cool.

Ranger Cookies
Makes 1 1/2 to 2 dozen

1 jar Ranger Cookie Mix
1/3 C. shortening
1 egg, slightly beaten

2 T. milk
1 tsp. vanilla

Preheat the oven to 375°F. In a large bowl, cream the shortening, egg, milk and vanilla. Add the Ranger Cookie Mix. Stir until the mixture is well blended. Drop by rounded teaspoonfuls 2 inches apart on an ungreased baking sheet. Bake for 8 to 9 minutes or until cookie edges are golden brown. Transfer to wire racks to cool.

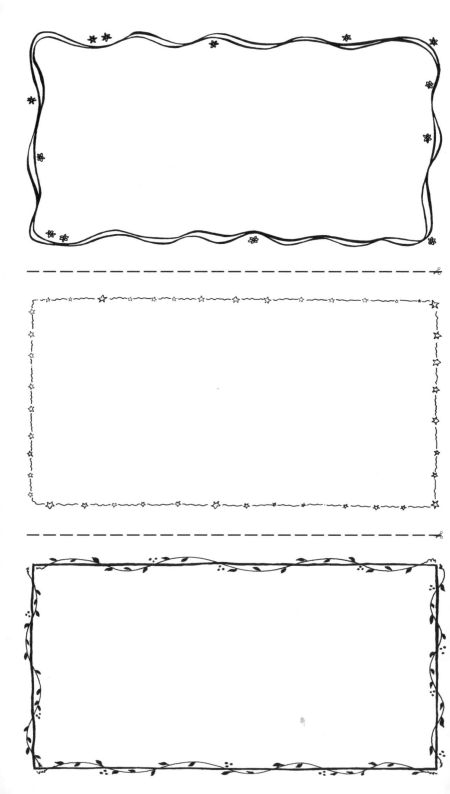

S'mores Squares Mix

1 sleeve of graham crackers
   reduced to crumbs
1/3 C. brown sugar
1 1/2 C. mini marshmallows
1 C. milk chocolate chips

Layer the ingredients in the order given into a wide-mouth 1-quart canning jar. Pack each layer in place before adding the next ingredient.

Attach a gift tag with the mixing and baking directions.

🌸 For a great kid gift, give one or two fun Gifts in a Jar wrapped in a child's apron. 🌸

S'mores Squares

Makes 9 to 12

1 jar S'mores Squares Mix
1/2 C. butter or margarine,
   melted
1 tsp. vanilla

Preheat the oven to 350°F. In a large bowl, place the S'mores Squares Mix. Pour the butter and vanilla over dry ingredients, mixing well. Pour into a greased 9-inch square pan. Bake for 15 minutes.

S'mores Squares

Makes 9 to 12

1 jar S'mores Squares Mix
1/2 C. butter or margarine,
  melted

1 tsp. vanilla

    Preheat the oven to 350°F. In a large bowl, place the S'mores Squares Mix. Pour the butter and vanilla over dry ingredients, mixing well. Pour into a greased 9-inch square pan. Bake for 15 minutes.

S'mores Squares

Makes 9 to 12

1 jar S'mores Squares Mix
1/2 C. butter or margarine,
  melted

1 tsp. vanilla

    Preheat the oven to 350°F. In a large bowl, place the S'mores Squares Mix. Pour the butter and vanilla over dry ingredients, mixing well. Pour into a greased 9-inch square pan. Bake for 15 minutes.

S'mores Squares

Makes 9 to 12

1 jar S'mores Squares Mix
1/2 C. butter or margarine,
  melted

1 tsp. vanilla

    Preheat the oven to 350°F. In a large bowl, place the S'mores Squares Mix. Pour the butter and vanilla over dry ingredients, mixing well. Pour into a greased 9-inch square pan. Bake for 15 minutes.

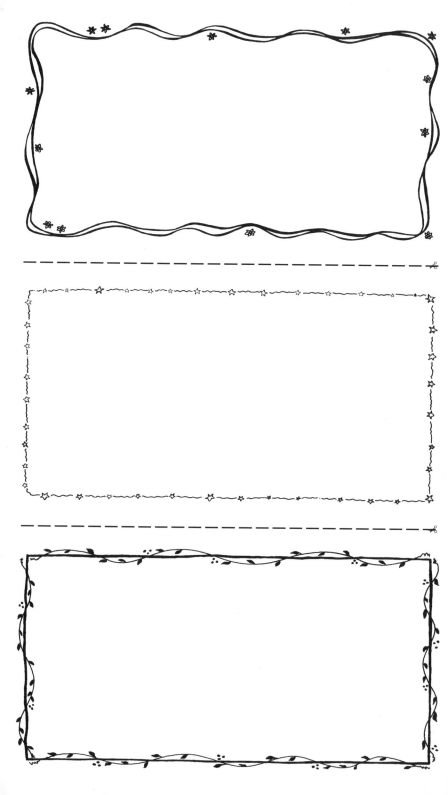

S'mores Squares

Makes 9 to 12

1 jar S'mores Squares Mix
1/2 C. butter or margarine,
  melted

1 tsp. vanilla

    Preheat the oven to 350°F. In a large bowl, place the S'mores Squares Mix. Pour the butter and vanilla over dry ingredients, mixing well. Pour into a greased 9-inch square pan. Bake for 15 minutes.

S'mores Squares

Makes 9 to 12

1 jar S'mores Squares Mix
1/2 C. butter or margarine,
  melted

1 tsp. vanilla

    Preheat the oven to 350°F. In a large bowl, place the S'mores Squares Mix. Pour the butter and vanilla over dry ingredients, mixing well. Pour into a greased 9-inch square pan. Bake for 15 minutes.

S'mores Squares

Makes 9 to 12

1 jar S'mores Squares Mix
1/2 C. butter or margarine,
  melted

1 tsp. vanilla

    Preheat the oven to 350°F. In a large bowl, place the S'mores Squares Mix. Pour the butter and vanilla over dry ingredients, mixing well. Pour into a greased 9-inch square pan. Bake for 15 minutes.

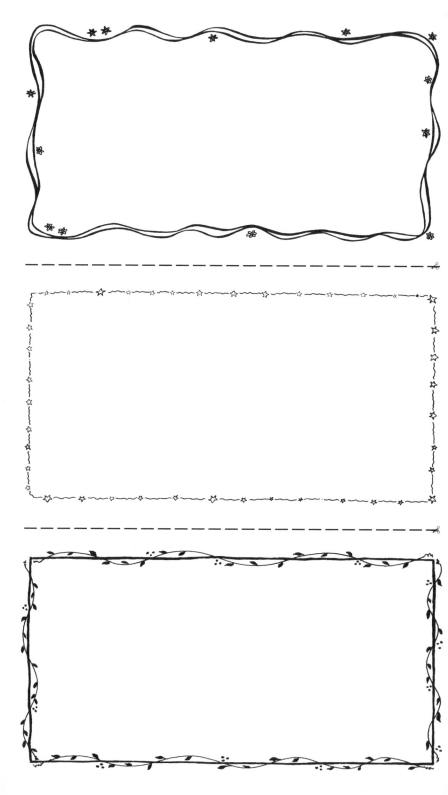

Funnel Cake Mix

4 C. all-purpose flour
3 T. plus 1 tsp. baking powder
1 tsp. salt
2 tsp. cinnamon

In a large bowl, combine the above ingredients and stir until the mixture is well blended. Place mix in a wide-mouth 1-quart canning jar.

Attach a gift tag with the mixing and frying directions.

❀ Small appliques or embroidery can be added to the center of a fabric cover to further personalize the gift. ❀

Funnel Cakes

Makes 16

For every 4 Funnel Cakes:
1 C. Funnel Cake Mix
1 egg
3/4 C. milk
Powdered sugar

Pour vegetable oil into a skillet to a depth of 1 inch. Heat oil to 360°F over medium high heat. In a small bowl, combine egg and milk. Add 1 cup Funnel Cake Mix and beat with fork until smooth. Holding finger under funnel opening, pour about 1/4 cup batter into funnel. Allow batter to pour from funnel into hot oil, moving funnel in a circle to form a spiral shape. Fry 1 minute, turn cake over and continue frying until golden brown. Remove to paper towel to drain. Sprinkle with powdered sugar.

Funnel Cakes
Makes 16

For every 4 Funnel Cakes:
1 C. Funnel Cake Mix
1 egg

3/4 C. milk
Powdered sugar

Pour vegetable oil into a skillet to a depth of 1 inch. Heat oil to 360°F over medium high heat. In a small bowl, combine egg and milk. Add 1 cup Funnel Cake Mix and beat with fork until smooth. Holding finger under funnel opening, pour about 1/4 cup batter into funnel. Allow batter to pour from funnel into hot oil, moving funnel in a circle to form a spiral shape. Fry 1 minute, turn cake over and continue frying until golden brown. Remove to paper towel to drain. Sprinkle with powdered sugar.

Funnel Cakes
Makes 16

For every 4 Funnel Cakes:
1 C. Funnel Cake Mix
1 egg

3/4 C. milk
Powdered sugar

Pour vegetable oil into a skillet to a depth of 1 inch. Heat oil to 360°F over medium high heat. In a small bowl, combine egg and milk. Add 1 cup Funnel Cake Mix and beat with fork until smooth. Holding finger under funnel opening, pour about 1/4 cup batter into funnel. Allow batter to pour from funnel into hot oil, moving funnel in a circle to form a spiral shape. Fry 1 minute, turn cake over and continue frying until golden brown. Remove to paper towel to drain. Sprinkle with powdered sugar.

Funnel Cakes
Makes 16

For every 4 Funnel Cakes:
1 C. Funnel Cake Mix
1 egg

3/4 C. milk
Powdered sugar

Pour vegetable oil into a skillet to a depth of 1 inch. Heat oil to 360°F over medium high heat. In a small bowl, combine egg and milk. Add 1 cup Funnel Cake Mix and beat with fork until smooth. Holding finger under funnel opening, pour about 1/4 cup batter into funnel. Allow batter to pour from funnel into hot oil, moving funnel in a circle to form a spiral shape. Fry 1 minute, turn cake over and continue frying until golden brown. Remove to paper towel to drain. Sprinkle with powdered sugar.

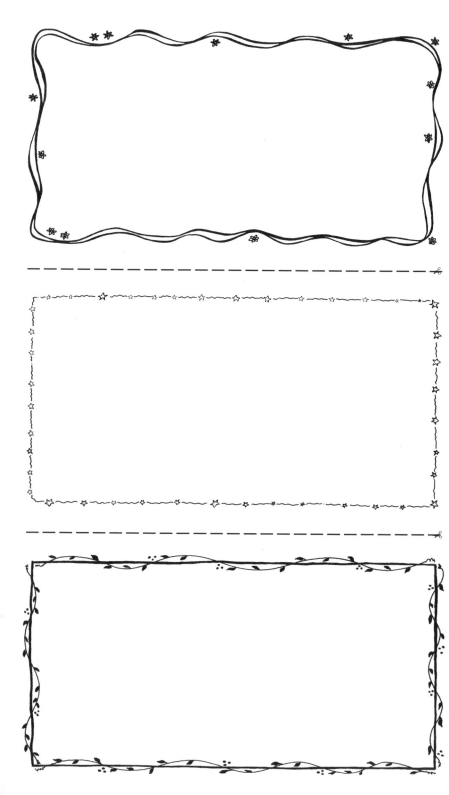

Funnel Cakes

Makes 16

For every 4 Funnel Cakes:

1 C. Funnel Cake Mix   3/4 C. milk
1 egg   Powdered sugar

Pour vegetable oil into a skillet to a depth of 1 inch. Heat oil to 360°F over medium high heat. In a small bowl, combine egg and milk. Add 1 cup Funnel Cake Mix and beat with fork until smooth. Holding finger under funnel opening, pour about 1/4 cup batter into funnel. Allow batter to pour from funnel into hot oil, moving funnel in a circle to form a spiral shape. Fry 1 minute, turn cake over and continue frying until golden brown. Remove to paper towel to drain. Sprinkle with powdered sugar.

Funnel Cakes

Makes 16

For every 4 Funnel Cakes:

1 C. Funnel Cake Mix   3/4 C. milk
1 egg   Powdered sugar

Pour vegetable oil into a skillet to a depth of 1 inch. Heat oil to 360°F over medium high heat. In a small bowl, combine egg and milk. Add 1 cup Funnel Cake Mix and beat with fork until smooth. Holding finger under funnel opening, pour about 1/4 cup batter into funnel. Allow batter to pour from funnel into hot oil, moving funnel in a circle to form a spiral shape. Fry 1 minute, turn cake over and continue frying until golden brown. Remove to paper towel to drain. Sprinkle with powdered sugar.

Funnel Cakes

Makes 16

For every 4 Funnel Cakes:

1 C. Funnel Cake Mix   3/4 C. milk
1 egg   Powdered sugar

Pour vegetable oil into a skillet to a depth of 1 inch. Heat oil to 360°F over medium high heat. In a small bowl, combine egg and milk. Add 1 cup Funnel Cake Mix and beat with fork until smooth. Holding finger under funnel opening, pour about 1/4 cup batter into funnel. Allow batter to pour from funnel into hot oil, moving funnel in a circle to form a spiral shape. Fry 1 minute, turn cake over and continue frying until golden brown. Remove to paper towel to drain. Sprinkle with powdered sugar.

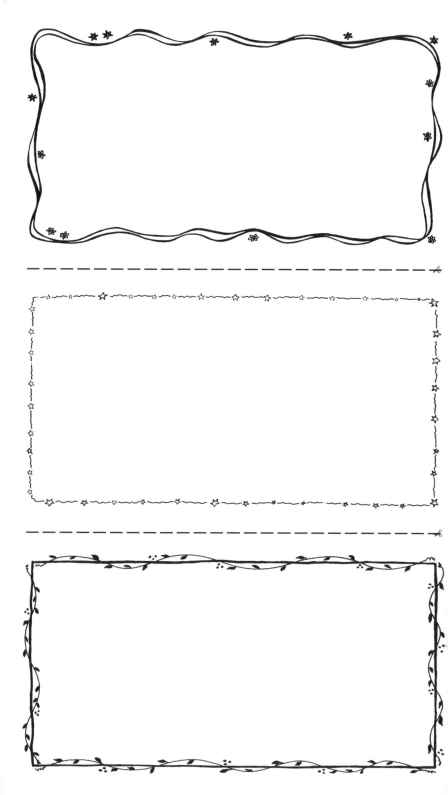

Trail Mix Bar Mix

1 1/4 C. quick oats
1/3 C. coarsely chopped walnuts
  or pecans
2/3 C. brown sugar
1/4 tsp. cinnamon
1/2 C. semi-sweet chocolate
  chips
1/2 C. baking and biscuit mix
1/3 C. dried cherries or raisins
1/4 C. shelled sunflower seeds

Layer the ingredients in the order given into a wide-mouth 1-quart canning jar. Pack each layer in place before adding the next ingredient.

Attach a gift tag with the mixing and baking directions.

Trail Mix Bars

Makes 9 to 12 bars

1 jar Trail Mix Bar Mix
1 egg, slightly beaten
2 T. milk
2 T. vegetable oil
1 tsp. vanilla

Preheat the oven to 375°F. In a large bowl, place the Trail Mix Bar Mix. Add egg, milk, oil and vanilla. Stir until the mixture is well blended. Spread into a greased 8-inch square baking pan. Bake for 25 minutes or until the edges are brown. Cool before cutting.

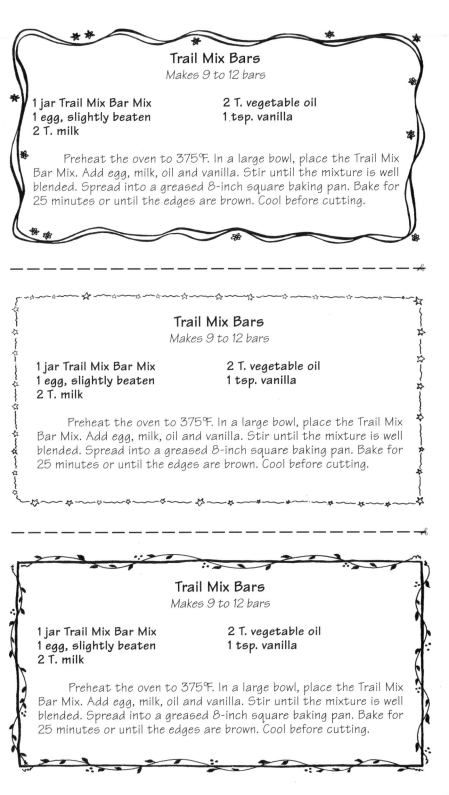

Trail Mix Bars
Makes 9 to 12 bars

1 jar Trail Mix Bar Mix
1 egg, slightly beaten
2 T. milk

2 T. vegetable oil
1 tsp. vanilla

Preheat the oven to 375°F. In a large bowl, place the Trail Mix Bar Mix. Add egg, milk, oil and vanilla. Stir until the mixture is well blended. Spread into a greased 8-inch square baking pan. Bake for 25 minutes or until the edges are brown. Cool before cutting.

Trail Mix Bars
Makes 9 to 12 bars

1 jar Trail Mix Bar Mix
1 egg, slightly beaten
2 T. milk

2 T. vegetable oil
1 tsp. vanilla

Preheat the oven to 375°F. In a large bowl, place the Trail Mix Bar Mix. Add egg, milk, oil and vanilla. Stir until the mixture is well blended. Spread into a greased 8-inch square baking pan. Bake for 25 minutes or until the edges are brown. Cool before cutting.

Trail Mix Bars
Makes 9 to 12 bars

1 jar Trail Mix Bar Mix
1 egg, slightly beaten
2 T. milk

2 T. vegetable oil
1 tsp. vanilla

Preheat the oven to 375°F. In a large bowl, place the Trail Mix Bar Mix. Add egg, milk, oil and vanilla. Stir until the mixture is well blended. Spread into a greased 8-inch square baking pan. Bake for 25 minutes or until the edges are brown. Cool before cutting.

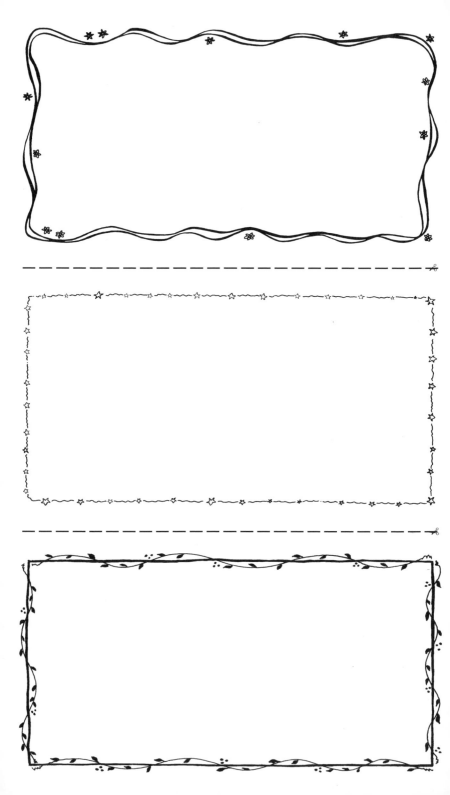

Trail Mix Bars
Makes 9 to 12 bars

1 jar Trail Mix Bar Mix
1 egg, slightly beaten
2 T. milk

2 T. vegetable oil
1 tsp. vanilla

Preheat the oven to 375°F. In a large bowl, place the Trail Mix Bar Mix. Add egg, milk, oil and vanilla. Stir until the mixture is well blended. Spread into a greased 8-inch square baking pan. Bake for 25 minutes or until the edges are brown. Cool before cutting.

Trail Mix Bars
Makes 9 to 12 bars

1 jar Trail Mix Bar Mix
1 egg, slightly beaten
2 T. milk

2 T. vegetable oil
1 tsp. vanilla

Preheat the oven to 375°F. In a large bowl, place the Trail Mix Bar Mix. Add egg, milk, oil and vanilla. Stir until the mixture is well blended. Spread into a greased 8-inch square baking pan. Bake for 25 minutes or until the edges are brown. Cool before cutting.

Trail Mix Bars
Makes 9 to 12 bars

1 jar Trail Mix Bar Mix
1 egg, slightly beaten
2 T. milk

2 T. vegetable oil
1 tsp. vanilla

Preheat the oven to 375°F. In a large bowl, place the Trail Mix Bar Mix. Add egg, milk, oil and vanilla. Stir until the mixture is well blended. Spread into a greased 8-inch square baking pan. Bake for 25 minutes or until the edges are brown. Cool before cutting.

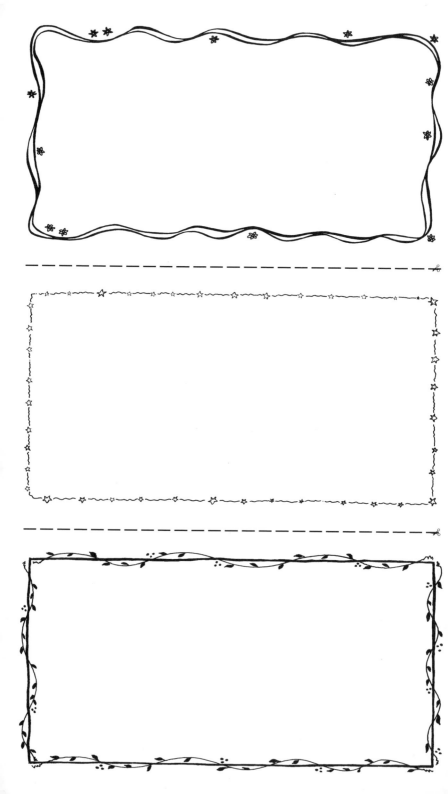

Chippers Mix

1/3 C. sugar
1 C. semi-sweet chocolate chips
1/2 C. peanut butter candy pieces
1/3 C. brown sugar
1 C. old-fashioned oats
3/4 C. all-purpose flour
1/2 tsp. baking soda

Layer the ingredients in the order given into a wide-mouth 1-quart canning jar. Pack each layer in place before adding the next ingredient.

Attach a gift tag with the mixing and baking directions.

Chippers

Makes 2 to 3 dozen

1 jar Chippers Mix
1/2 C. butter or margarine,
   softened
1 egg, slightly beaten
1 tsp. vanilla

Preheat the oven to 375°F. In a large bowl, cream the butter, egg and vanilla. Add the Chippers Mix. Stir until the mixture is well blended. Drop heaping teaspoonfuls 2 inches apart on an ungreased cookie sheet. Bake for 9 to 12 minutes or until the cookie edges are lightly browned. Transfer to wire racks to cool.

Chippers

Makes 2 to 3 dozen

1 jar Chippers Mix
1/2 C. butter or margarine,
  softened

1 egg, slightly beaten
1 tsp. vanilla

    Preheat the oven to 375°F. In a large bowl, cream the butter, egg and vanilla. Add the Chippers Mix. Stir until the mixture is well blended. Drop heaping teaspoonfuls 2 inches apart on an ungreased cookie sheet. Bake for 9 to 12 minutes or until the cookie edges are lightly browned. Transfer to wire racks to cool.

Chippers

Makes 2 to 3 dozen

1 jar Chippers Mix
1/2 C. butter or margarine,
  softened

1 egg, slightly beaten
1 tsp. vanilla

    Preheat the oven to 375°F. In a large bowl, cream the butter, egg and vanilla. Add the Chippers Mix. Stir until the mixture is well blended. Drop heaping teaspoonfuls 2 inches apart on an ungreased cookie sheet. Bake for 9 to 12 minutes or until the cookie edges are lightly browned. Transfer to wire racks to cool.

Chippers

Makes 2 to 3 dozen

1 jar Chippers Mix
1/2 C. butter or margarine,
  softened

1 egg, slightly beaten
1 tsp. vanilla

    Preheat the oven to 375°F. In a large bowl, cream the butter, egg and vanilla. Add the Chippers Mix. Stir until the mixture is well blended. Drop heaping teaspoonfuls 2 inches apart on an ungreased cookie sheet. Bake for 9 to 12 minutes or until the cookie edges are lightly browned. Transfer to wire racks to cool.

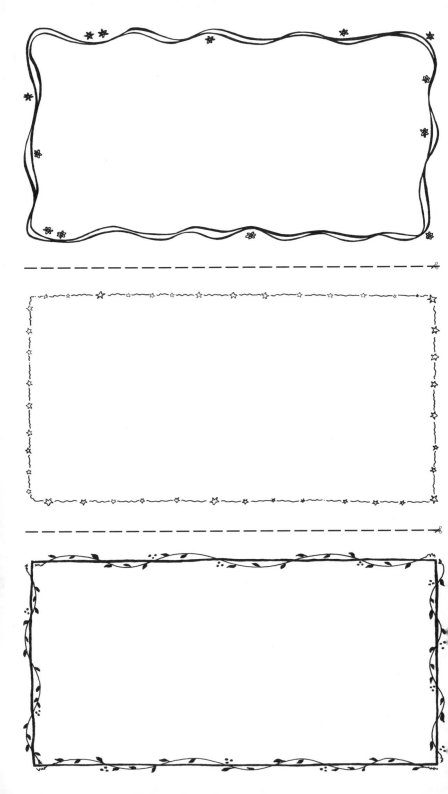

Chippers

Makes 2 to 3 dozen

1 jar Chippers Mix
1/2 C. butter or margarine,
  softened

1 egg, slightly beaten
1 tsp. vanilla

Preheat the oven to 375°F. In a large bowl, cream the butter, egg and vanilla. Add the Chippers Mix. Stir until the mixture is well blended. Drop heaping teaspoonfuls 2 inches apart on an ungreased cookie sheet. Bake for 9 to 12 minutes or until the cookie edges are lightly browned. Transfer to wire racks to cool.

Chippers

Makes 2 to 3 dozen

1 jar Chippers Mix
1/2 C. butter or margarine,
  softened

1 egg, slightly beaten
1 tsp. vanilla

Preheat the oven to 375°F. In a large bowl, cream the butter, egg and vanilla. Add the Chippers Mix. Stir until the mixture is well blended. Drop heaping teaspoonfuls 2 inches apart on an ungreased cookie sheet. Bake for 9 to 12 minutes or until the cookie edges are lightly browned. Transfer to wire racks to cool.

Chippers

Makes 2 to 3 dozen

1 jar Chippers Mix
1/2 C. butter or margarine,
  softened

1 egg, slightly beaten
1 tsp. vanilla

Preheat the oven to 375°F. In a large bowl, cream the butter, egg and vanilla. Add the Chippers Mix. Stir until the mixture is well blended. Drop heaping teaspoonfuls 2 inches apart on an ungreased cookie sheet. Bake for 9 to 12 minutes or until the cookie edges are lightly browned. Transfer to wire racks to cool.

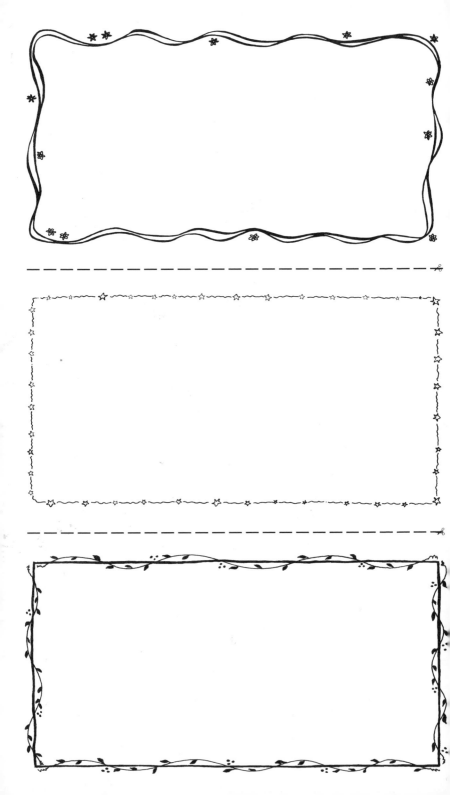

Friendship Brownie Mix

2/3 C. sugar
1/2 C. vanilla chips
1/2 C. semi-sweet chocolate
   chips
1/2 C. walnuts
2/3 C. brown sugar
1/3 C. unsweetened cocoa
1 C. all-purpose flour
1 tsp. baking soda
1/2 tsp. salt

Layer the ingredients in the order given into a wide-mouth 1-quart canning jar. Pack each layer in place before adding the next ingredient.

Attach a gift tag with the mixing and baking directions.

❀ For a special touch, attach a wooden spoon to the jar. ❀

Friendship Brownies

1 jar Friendship Brownie Mix
3 eggs
2/3 C. vegetable oil
1 tsp. vanilla

Preheat the oven to 350°F. In a large bowl, cream the eggs, oil and vanilla. Add the Friendship Brownie Mix. Stir until the mixture is well blended. Spread in a greased 9-inch square baking pan. Bake for 34 to 38 minutes or until a toothpick inserted in the center comes out clean. Cool before cutting.

Double Fudge Brownie Mix

2 C. sugar
1/2 C. unsweetened cocoa (clean
    inside of jar with a paper towel
    after this layer)
1 C. all-purpose flour
1/2 C. chopped pecans
1/2 C. chocolate chips

Layer the ingredients in the order given into a wide-mouth 1-quart canning jar. Pack each layer in place before adding the next ingredient.

Attach a gift tag with the mixing and baking directions.

Double Fudge Brownies

1 jar Double Fudge Brownie Mix
1 C. butter or margarine,
   softened
4 eggs

Preheat the oven to 325°F. In a large bowl, cream the butter. Add the eggs, one at a time, beating well after each egg. Add the Double Fudge Brownie Mix and continue to beat the mixture until it is smooth. Spread the mixture into a greased 9 x 12 inch baking pan. Bake for 40 to 50 minutes. Cool before cutting.

Double Fudge Brownies

1 jar Double Fudge Brownie Mix   4 eggs
1 C. butter or margarine,
   softened

   Preheat the oven to 325°F. In a large bowl, cream the butter.
Add the eggs, one at a time, beating well after each egg. Add the
Double Fudge Brownie Mix and continue to beat the mixture until it
is smooth. Spread the mixture into a greased 9 x 12 inch baking
pan. Bake for 40 to 50 minutes. Cool before cutting.

Double Fudge Brownies

1 jar Double Fudge Brownie Mix   4 eggs
1 C. butter or margarine,
   softened

   Preheat the oven to 325°F. In a large bowl, cream the butter.
Add the eggs, one at a time, beating well after each egg. Add the
Double Fudge Brownie Mix and continue to beat the mixture until it
is smooth. Spread the mixture into a greased 9 x 12 inch baking
pan. Bake for 40 to 50 minutes. Cool before cutting.

Double Fudge Brownies

1 jar Double Fudge Brownie Mix   4 eggs
1 C. butter or margarine,
   softened

   Preheat the oven to 325°F. In a large bowl, cream the butter.
Add the eggs, one at a time, beating well after each egg. Add the
Double Fudge Brownie Mix and continue to beat the mixture until it
is smooth. Spread the mixture into a greased 9 x 12 inch baking
pan. Bake for 40 to 50 minutes. Cool before cutting.

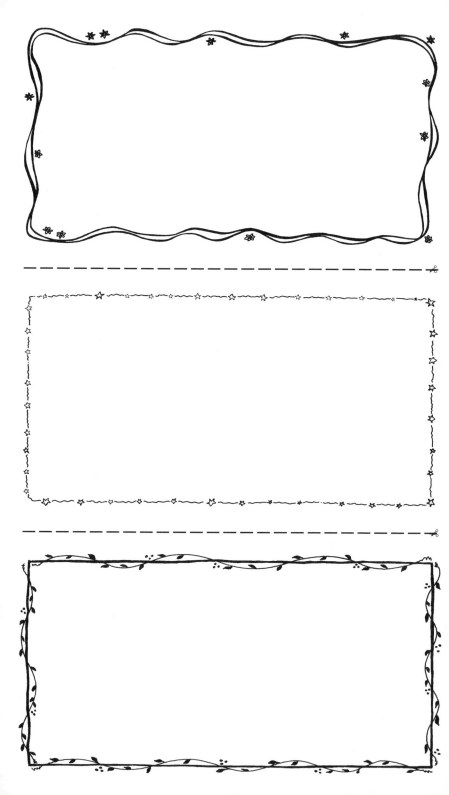

Double Fudge Brownies

1 jar Double Fudge Brownie Mix   4 eggs
1 C. butter or margarine,
  softened

    Preheat the oven to 325°F. In a large bowl, cream the butter. Add the eggs, one at a time, beating well after each egg. Add the Double Fudge Brownie Mix and continue to beat the mixture until it is smooth. Spread the mixture into a greased 9 x 12 inch baking pan. Bake for 40 to 50 minutes. Cool before cutting.

Double Fudge Brownies

1 jar Double Fudge Brownie Mix   4 eggs
1 C. butter or margarine,
  softened

    Preheat the oven to 325°F. In a large bowl, cream the butter. Add the eggs, one at a time, beating well after each egg. Add the Double Fudge Brownie Mix and continue to beat the mixture until it is smooth. Spread the mixture into a greased 9 x 12 inch baking pan. Bake for 40 to 50 minutes. Cool before cutting.

Double Fudge Brownies

1 jar Double Fudge Brownie Mix   4 eggs
1 C. butter or margarine,
  softened

    Preheat the oven to 325°F. In a large bowl, cream the butter. Add the eggs, one at a time, beating well after each egg. Add the Double Fudge Brownie Mix and continue to beat the mixture until it is smooth. Spread the mixture into a greased 9 x 12 inch baking pan. Bake for 40 to 50 minutes. Cool before cutting.

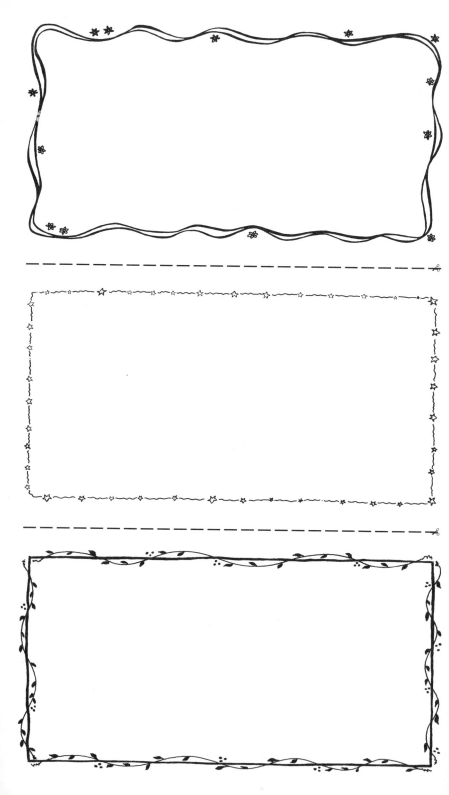

Puppy Chow Mix

1/3 C. semi-sweet chocolate chips (placed in a plain baggie)
3 1/4 C. bite-size rice squares cereal
1/2 C. powdered sugar (placed in a sealed baggie)

Layer the ingredients in the order given into a wide-mouth 1-quart canning jar. Pack each layer in place before adding the next ingredient.

Attach a gift tag with the mixing directions.

Puppy Chow

1 jar Puppy Chow Mix
3 T. peanut butter

Remove powdered sugar and set aside. Remove cereal from jar and place into a large bowl. Place chocolate chips in a small microwave safe dish and add peanut butter. Microwave on high for 30 seconds. Stir. Continue to microwave mixture for 15 seconds at a time, stirring each time until the chips are completely melted and the mixture is smooth. Pour mixture over cereal and stir gently until the cereal is well coated. Add powdered sugar a little at a time, stir and continue to add until well coated. Spread Puppy Chow into a single layer and allow to dry. Store in an airtight container.

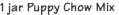

Puppy Chow

1 jar Puppy Chow Mix   **3 T. peanut butter**

Remove powdered sugar and set aside. Remove cereal from jar and place into a large bowl. Place chocolate chips in a small microwave safe dish and add peanut butter. Microwave on high for 30 seconds. Stir. Continue to microwave mixture for 15 seconds at a time, stirring each time until the chips are completely melted and the mixture is smooth. Pour mixture over cereal and stir gently until the cereal is well coated. Add powdered sugar a little at a time, stir and continue to add until well coated. Spread Puppy Chow into a single layer and allow to dry. Store in an airtight container.

Puppy Chow

1 jar Puppy Chow Mix   **3 T. peanut butter**

Remove powdered sugar and set aside. Remove cereal from jar and place into a large bowl. Place chocolate chips in a small microwave safe dish and add peanut butter. Microwave on high for 30 seconds. Stir. Continue to microwave mixture for 15 seconds at a time, stirring each time until the chips are completely melted and the mixture is smooth. Pour mixture over cereal and stir gently until the cereal is well coated. Add powdered sugar a little at a time, stir and continue to add until well coated. Spread Puppy Chow into a single layer and allow to dry. Store in an airtight container.

Puppy Chow

1 jar Puppy Chow Mix   **3 T. peanut butter**

Remove powdered sugar and set aside. Remove cereal from jar and place into a large bowl. Place chocolate chips in a small microwave safe dish and add peanut butter. Microwave on high for 30 seconds. Stir. Continue to microwave mixture for 15 seconds at a time, stirring each time until the chips are completely melted and the mixture is smooth. Pour mixture over cereal and stir gently until the cereal is well coated. Add powdered sugar a little at a time, stir and continue to add until well coated. Spread Puppy Chow into a single layer and allow to dry. Store in an airtight container.

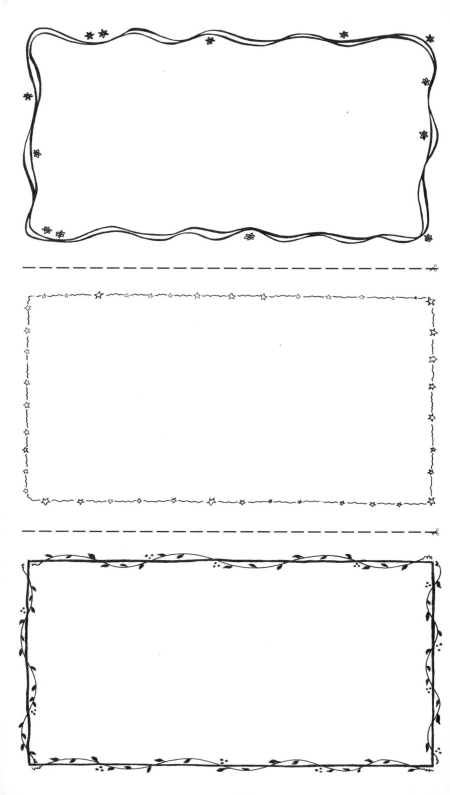

Puppy Chow

1 jar Puppy Chow Mix   3 T. peanut butter

Remove powdered sugar and set aside. Remove cereal from jar and place into a large bowl. Place chocolate chips in a small microwave safe dish and add peanut butter. Microwave on high for 30 seconds. Stir. Continue to microwave mixture for 15 seconds at a time, stirring each time until the chips are completely melted and the mixture is smooth. Pour mixture over cereal and stir gently until the cereal is well coated. Add powdered sugar a little at a time, stir and continue to add until well coated. Spread Puppy Chow into a single layer and allow to dry. Store in an airtight container.

Puppy Chow

1 jar Puppy Chow Mix   3 T. peanut butter

Remove powdered sugar and set aside. Remove cereal from jar and place into a large bowl. Place chocolate chips in a small microwave safe dish and add peanut butter. Microwave on high for 30 seconds. Stir. Continue to microwave mixture for 15 seconds at a time, stirring each time until the chips are completely melted and the mixture is smooth. Pour mixture over cereal and stir gently until the cereal is well coated. Add powdered sugar a little at a time, stir and continue to add until well coated. Spread Puppy Chow into a single layer and allow to dry. Store in an airtight container.

Puppy Chow

1 jar Puppy Chow Mix   3 T. peanut butter

Remove powdered sugar and set aside. Remove cereal from jar and place into a large bowl. Place chocolate chips in a small microwave safe dish and add peanut butter. Microwave on high for 30 seconds. Stir. Continue to microwave mixture for 15 seconds at a time, stirring each time until the chips are completely melted and the mixture is smooth. Pour mixture over cereal and stir gently until the cereal is well coated. Add powdered sugar a little at a time, stir and continue to add until well coated. Spread Puppy Chow into a single layer and allow to dry. Store in an airtight container.

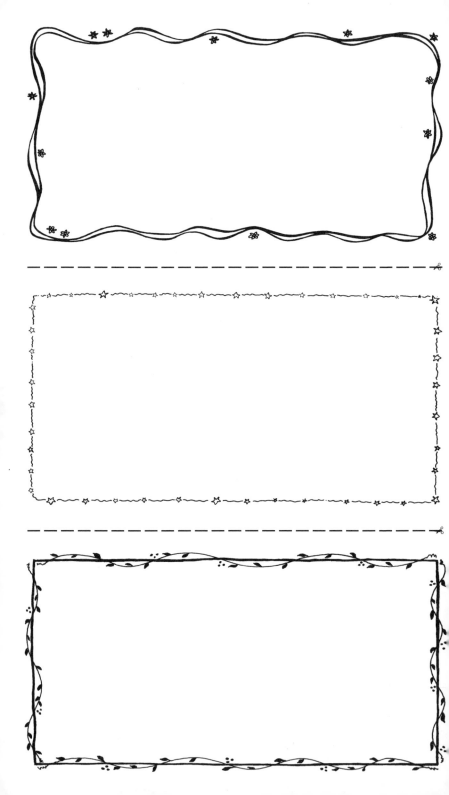

Dirt Cups Mix

1 large box instant chocolate
    pudding (without packaging)
16 gummy worms
16 Oreo cookies, crushed and
    placed into one or two baggies

Layer the ingredients in the order given into a wide-mouth 1-quart canning jar. Pack each layer in place before adding the next ingredient.

Attach a gift tag with the mixing directions.

Dirt Cups

Makes 8 servings

1 jar Dirt Cups Mix
4 C. cold milk
1 C. whipped topping

Remove Oreos from jar. Set aside. In a large bowl, place the rest of the Dirt Cups Mix. Remove worms and set aside. Add milk and mix well. Place in refrigerator until set. When set, add whipped topping and stir. Place 1 tablespoon of crushed cookies in the bottoms of 8 paper cups. Split pudding mixture evenly between the eight cups. Top each cup with the remaining cookies. Garnish Dirt Cups with gummy worms.

Dirt Cups
Makes 8 servings

1 jar Dirt Cups Mix   **1 C. whipped topping**
4 C. cold milk

Remove Oreos from jar. Set aside. In a large bowl, place the rest of the Dirt Cups Mix. Remove worms and set aside. Add milk and mix well. Place in refrigerator until set. When set, add whipped topping and stir. Place 1 tablespoon of crushed cookies in the bottoms of 8 paper cups. Split pudding mixture evenly between the eight cups. Top each cup with the remaining cookies. Garnish Dirt Cups with gummy worms.

Dirt Cups
Makes 8 servings

1 jar Dirt Cups Mix   **1 C. whipped topping**
4 C. cold milk

Remove Oreos from jar. Set aside. In a large bowl, place the rest of the Dirt Cups Mix. Remove worms and set aside. Add milk and mix well. Place in refrigerator until set. When set, add whipped topping and stir. Place 1 tablespoon of crushed cookies in the bottoms of 8 paper cups. Split pudding mixture evenly between the eight cups. Top each cup with the remaining cookies. Garnish Dirt Cups with gummy worms.

Dirt Cups
Makes 8 servings

1 jar Dirt Cups Mix   **1 C. whipped topping**
4 C. cold milk

Remove Oreos from jar. Set aside. In a large bowl, place the rest of the Dirt Cups Mix. Remove worms and set aside. Add milk and mix well. Place in refrigerator until set. When set, add whipped topping and stir. Place 1 tablespoon of crushed cookies in the bottoms of 8 paper cups. Split pudding mixture evenly between the eight cups. Top each cup with the remaining cookies. Garnish Dirt Cups with gummy worms.

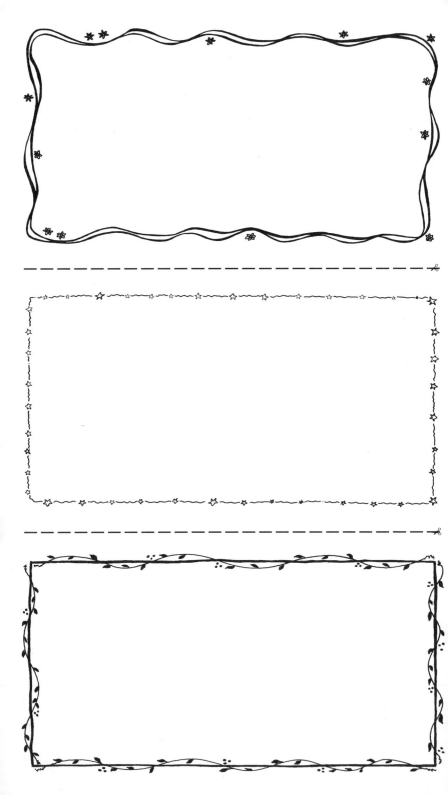

Dirt Cups
Makes 8 servings

1 jar Dirt Cups Mix   1 C. whipped topping
4 C. cold milk

Remove Oreos from jar. Set aside. In a large bowl, place the rest of the Dirt Cups Mix. Remove worms and set aside. Add milk and mix well. Place in refrigerator until set. When set, add whipped topping and stir. Place 1 tablespoon of crushed cookies in the bottoms of 8 paper cups. Split pudding mixture evenly between the eight cups. Top each cup with the remaining cookies. Garnish Dirt Cups with gummy worms.

Dirt Cups
Makes 8 servings

1 jar Dirt Cups Mix   1 C. whipped topping
4 C. cold milk

Remove Oreos from jar. Set aside. In a large bowl, place the rest of the Dirt Cups Mix. Remove worms and set aside. Add milk and mix well. Place in refrigerator until set. When set, add whipped topping and stir. Place 1 tablespoon of crushed cookies in the bottoms of 8 paper cups. Split pudding mixture evenly between the eight cups. Top each cup with the remaining cookies. Garnish Dirt Cups with gummy worms.

Dirt Cups
Makes 8 servings

1 jar Dirt Cups Mix   1 C. whipped topping
4 C. cold milk

Remove Oreos from jar. Set aside. In a large bowl, place the rest of the Dirt Cups Mix. Remove worms and set aside. Add milk and mix well. Place in refrigerator until set. When set, add whipped topping and stir. Place 1 tablespoon of crushed cookies in the bottoms of 8 paper cups. Split pudding mixture evenly between the eight cups. Top each cup with the remaining cookies. Garnish Dirt Cups with gummy worms.

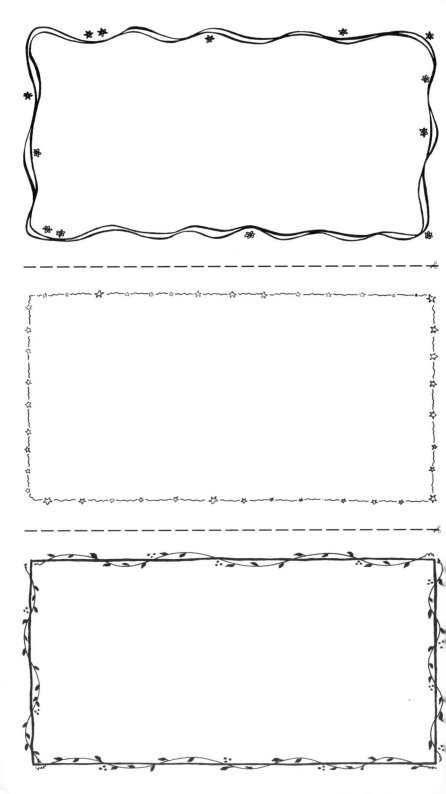

Play Dough Mix

2 C. all-purpose flour
1 C. salt
2 T. cream of tartar
2 packages of Kool-Aid
(leave in packaging)

Layer the ingredients in the order given into a wide-mouth 1-quart canning jar. Pack each layer in place before adding the next ingredient.

Attach a gift tag with the mixing directions.

❀ *To make a gift in a jar fancier, decorate it with a doily and ribbon.* ❀

Play Dough

1 jar Play Dough Mix
2 C. water
2 T. baby oil

Remove Kool-Aid packages from jar. Mix water, baby oil and Kool-Aid together in a large microwave safe container. Add Play Dough Mix and stir until well blended. Microwave on high for a total of approximately 4 to 5 minutes, stopping every 30 to 45 seconds to stir. Continue to microwave and stir until a ball forms. After the play dough is cool enough to touch, you're ready to play!

Play Dough

1 jar Play Dough Mix   **2 T. baby oil**
2 C. water

Remove Kool-Aid packages from jar. Mix water, baby oil and Kool-Aid together in a large microwave safe container. Add Play Dough Mix and stir until well blended. Microwave on high for a total of approximately 4 to 5 minutes, stopping every 30 to 45 seconds to stir. Continue to microwave and stir until a ball forms. After the play dough is cool enough to touch, you're ready to play!

Play Dough

1 jar Play Dough Mix   **2 T. baby oil**
2 C. water

Remove Kool-Aid packages from jar. Mix water, baby oil and Kool-Aid together in a large microwave safe container. Add Play Dough Mix and stir until well blended. Microwave on high for a total of approximately 4 to 5 minutes, stopping every 30 to 45 seconds to stir. Continue to microwave and stir until a ball forms. After the play dough is cool enough to touch, you're ready to play!

Play Dough

1 jar Play Dough Mix   **2 T. baby oil**
2 C. water

Remove Kool-Aid packages from jar. Mix water, baby oil and Kool-Aid together in a large microwave safe container. Add Play Dough Mix and stir until well blended. Microwave on high for a total of approximately 4 to 5 minutes, stopping every 30 to 45 seconds to stir. Continue to microwave and stir until a ball forms. After the play dough is cool enough to touch, you're ready to play!

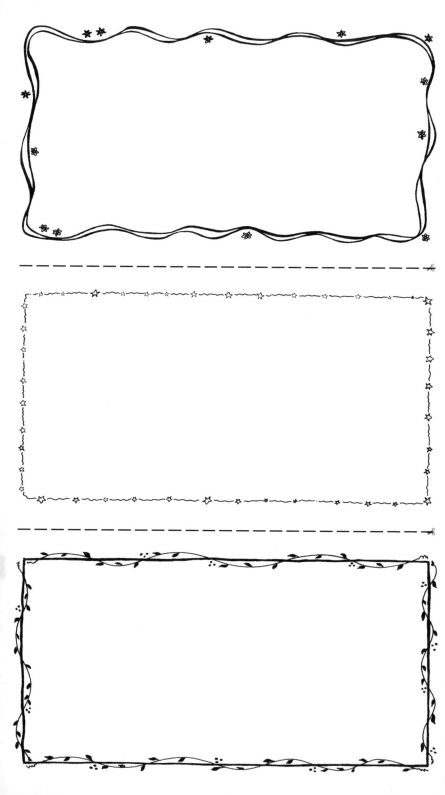

Play Dough

1 jar Play Dough Mix
2 C. water

2 T. baby oil

Remove Kool-Aid packages from jar. Mix water, baby oil and Kool-Aid together in a large microwave safe container. Add Play Dough Mix and stir until well blended. Microwave on high for a total of approximately 4 to 5 minutes, stopping every 30 to 45 seconds to stir. Continue to microwave and stir until a ball forms. After the play dough is cool enough to touch, you're ready to play!

Play Dough

1 jar Play Dough Mix
2 C. water

2 T. baby oil

Remove Kool-Aid packages from jar. Mix water, baby oil and Kool-Aid together in a large microwave safe container. Add Play Dough Mix and stir until well blended. Microwave on high for a total of approximately 4 to 5 minutes, stopping every 30 to 45 seconds to stir. Continue to microwave and stir until a ball forms. After the play dough is cool enough to touch, you're ready to play!

Play Dough

1 jar Play Dough Mix
2 C. water

2 T. baby oil

Remove Kool-Aid packages from jar. Mix water, baby oil and Kool-Aid together in a large microwave safe container. Add Play Dough Mix and stir until well blended. Microwave on high for a total of approximately 4 to 5 minutes, stopping every 30 to 45 seconds to stir. Continue to microwave and stir until a ball forms. After the play dough is cool enough to touch, you're ready to play!

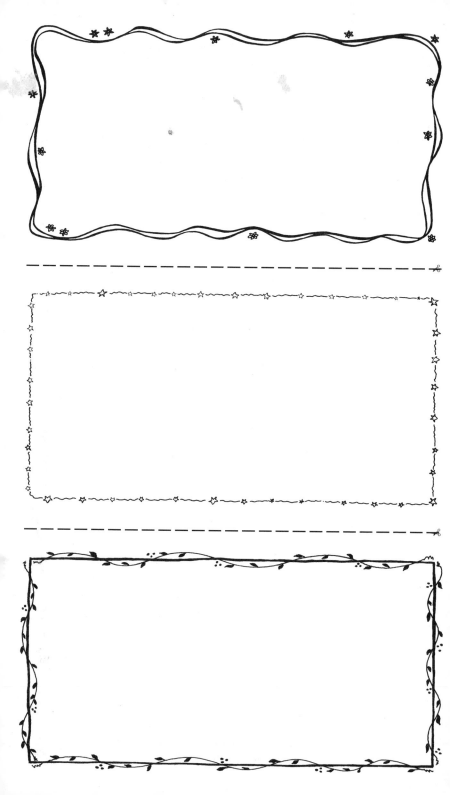

Gone Fishin' Munchin' Mix

1 C. bite-size pretzel goldfish crackers

1 C. bite-size corn squares cereal

1 C. bite-size original goldfish crackers

1 C. cocktail peanuts

Layer the ingredients in the order given into a wide-mouth 1-quart canning jar. Pack each layer in place before adding the next ingredient.

Attach a gift tag with the mixing and baking directions.

Gone Fishin' Munchin' Mix

1 jar Gone Fishin' Munchin' Mix
2 1/2 T. butter or margarine
2 1/2 tsp. Worcestershire
  sauce
1 tsp. powdered BBQ
  seasoning

Preheat the oven to 250°F. Empty contents of jar into a bowl, stirring to combine. Melt butter in a small saucepan over low heat. Stir in Worcestershire sauce and BBQ seasoning. Pour butter mixture over snack mixture. Stir to evenly coat snack mixture. Spread coated mixture in a single layer on cookie sheet. Bake for 45 minutes, stirring mixture every 15 minutes. When baking is completed, remove pan from oven and spread mixture in a single layer on a paper towel to cool. Store in an airtight container.